Finance for the Terrified

Finance for the Terrified

by

Mike Grace, BDS, DGDP (UK)

Editor, British Dental Journal,
64 Wimpole Street, London W1M 8AL

Series Editor
Fiona Stuart-Wilson, MA (Cantab), Assoc. IPD, MIMC CMC

Published by the British Dental Association
64 Wimpole Street, London W1M 8AL

Based on articles printed in Dental Business,
a supplement to the British Dental Journal

© British Dental Journal 1998

ISBN 0 904 58852 1

Printed and bound in Great Britain by
Latimer Trend, Plymouth, UK

Preface

Financial management either fascinates people or terrifies them. Unlike money itself (which virtually everyone is interested in) the management of money is something people approach with cautious apprehension— if they approach it at all. Understanding the management of your business finances (especially when you own the business) is even more important because the consequences of poor financial management in business can have a devastating effect on your personal financial fortune and the lives of others, for example the people you employ. Yet, despite the dangers of neglecting the financial side of the business, many sole traders (and quite a few large corporations as well) place the financial tasks necessary low down in their priorities, preferring the 'sexier' subjects of marketing, customer care and product development. Perhaps this is especially true in dentistry, where traditionally the commercial aspects of finance have been regarded with some disdain (and even antagonism). In the past many dentists seemed to see a conflict between ethical patient care and financial acumen, as if maximising profit was only possible at the expense of good clinical care.

If you are one of the many who feel 'bewitched' by financial terminology, 'bothered' by your accounts and 'bewildered' by pages of figures, then this book is for you. It is based on a series of articles I wrote for *Dental Business*, the business supplement to the *British Dental Journal*, in 1996 and 1997 for people who felt absolutely 'terrified' by the mysteries of financial accounting and for whom the terms 'balance sheet' and 'depreciation' were as inexplicable as nuclear physics is to the average person. I wrote it because I was once one of the 'terrified' myself, and had been as ignorant of financial concepts when I was working in general dental practice, even though I was a principal in a group practice with my own financial responsibilities.

I believe, from the many comments I have had from people who read the original series in *Dental Business*, that this book explains the basic principles of finance in a way that makes money understandable to even the most 'financially terrified'. At all times I have provided the really relevant points of financial management to dental practice when discussing the concepts or explaining what a financial term means.

By the time you have finished the book I hope you agree with me that finance can be a fascinating subject. It is definitely an important subject. This book should not only help you understand what your accountant is talking about, it should give you the confidence to make better and more informed financial decisions for the benefit of yourself and your practice.

I would especially like to acknowledge the help of Teresa Waddington, Leslie Smillie and Karen Frazer, the assistant editors at the BDJ office who improved my words and designed the pages for the original articles.

Mike Grace
September 1997

Contents

Introduction

These days health care professionals are being asked to behave even more ethically, to regulate themselves even more, to be attentive to the consumer-led society, and to run effective and profitable businesses.

For some people, these expectations from society are not only difficult, but threatening to the ethics of the profession itself. How can you maximise the profit in your business and behave ethically? How can you combine self-regulation with effective management techniques? Surely professional advice to meet clinical needs and patient demands will conflict?

I believe these questions reveal a lack of understanding of how ethical behaviour, customer care (the non-clinical aspects of patient care) and good business principles can work together to enhance each other and provide a better quality of dentistry as well as a better working environment for all the dental team.

Part of the synergy between clinical dental care and the business side of dentistry is the security of a firm financial base for the organisation. If the finances are running smoothly then the whole dental team can focus their energies on the patient care. If there is a financial problem then it begins to infiltrate the day-to-day running of the practice. More significantly, financial problems tend to infiltrate our other activities as we worry more and more about them. Thus, good financial management is an essential part of the management of a dental practice, and increasing in importance in dental clinics, hospitals and other organisations.

Good financial management is not difficult, even for the 'financially impaired' (those of us whose eyes glaze over at the mention of gross versus net, turnover versus profit, compound interest and APR, and other mystical terms). Money is simply a method of exchange we have chosen to make basic business (the exchange of goods and services that are valued) easier to transact. You offer me a service (or product) which I value, so I pay you. I offer a different service (or product) to someone else who pays me so I can purchase further services from you. In order that I keep myself safe and secure I must ensure I continue to get paid in

1

advance of my requirements to purchase from others. Put simply, make sure the money coming in balances the money going out.

If financial life was always that simple we would not need this book, nor the accountant. Unfortunately society is a little more complex nowadays. Part of our exchange system (the fact that we use money) is with governments who produce a whole array of different tax systems, and with banks who keep our money safe and charge us for it. Part of our exchange system involves attempts by others to extract as much money as possible from us and our attempts to reduce this as much as possible. Part of our exchange system involves borrowing in advance or investing (both neat ploys to sell more and charge us interest for doing it). Finance itself has become a mass of rules and conventions, and systems that have been created to try and make sure the rules are fair and we all play this sophisticated game of exchange legally.

Whether we like it or not, we have to live by the accepted conventions of today and rely on accountants, auditors and other financial experts to represent our interests in this maelstrom. As others rely on us to give them help with their oral health, so we rely on others to help us with our financial health. But advisers can only advise. They cannot make our decisions for us, and if they do they will make assumptions about us that may be incorrect. Imagine your solicitor deciding how to split up your estate in your will, or your garage mechanic deciding whether you should use your car to drive to work.

In finance we may initially be tempted to allow our adviser to make our financial decisions for us because we do not understand enough about the concepts. But we are not completely helpless. We can learn enough of the basics to make our own decisions on what we want to do, and to provide guidance to our advisers over those decisions. This book will help you do just that.

The business owner should know the business's financial situation at any moment in time, and whether the business profits are growing or shrinking. The two basic financial tools that provide this information are the balance sheet and the profit and loss account (P & L). These two documents tell you where you are now in your business and how well or badly the business is doing. I will explain them both in Chapter 2, focusing on the balance sheet in Chapter 2 and the profit and loss account in Chapter 3.

Some financial concepts are misunderstood by people, and depreciation is one of the most common. Accountants tend to put mysterious figures into P & L accounts and label them 'depreciation'. Most people only know that these figures help reduce the tax liability by reducing the profits. However, depreciation is far more than just a 'tax dodge', and Chapter 4 explains what it is, how it is worked out, and why it is something you should understand.

Looking ahead in business is just as important as analysing the past—some would say more important. Chapter 5 looks at budgeting in depth, especially at the use of a cash flow forecast in dental practice.

Finally Chapter 6 covers an aspect of finance that is often neglected in dental business—profit. While profit must never be the sole aim of any business at the expense of all other things, profit is the main aim for every business. Without profit a business will fail, and if you cannot make enough profit then you could do better by investing the start up costs of the business in a bank or investment account. Chapter 6 looks at getting the balance right, and what measures you can take to improve profitability without sacrificing your ethics.

If this book helps you communicate with your accountant with a better understanding then it will have served its purpose well. If this book also helps you plan for a better financial future I will be delighted. Even if all this book does is sit on the shelf for quick reference every time you receive your annual accounts, then it will have helped a little.

Finance is the life-blood of any business. Good financial health has so many benefits for the people working within the business and the customers that business serves. Good financial management not only provides satisfaction for the owner, but better return in financial terms as well. What more could you ask?

1

Financial principles

Managing money is one of the key elements of controlling a business. Indeed a lack of good financial planning is one of the most common reasons why businesses fail. When a business is in trouble, the first thing a consultant will look at is the financial situation. If it is not possible to save the business financially, no matter how good the product, how attractive the market and how motivated and experienced the people, the consultant will advise the company is closed down. Money really is the bottom line.

Finance and healthcare

In traditional healthcare, money is often either an awkward embarrassment or dismissed by the doctors, nurses and other clinical staff as irrelevant to the 'real' business of caring for patients. In dentistry, however, dentists have always had to combine the commercial reality of running a business with the professional aspects of providing quality dental care.

In the past most dentists have enjoyed a sellers' market that has enabled them to set up a dental practice without paying too much attention to the business side, and not only survive, but do very well in comparison with most other small businesses. In many countries around the world now those days are ending with the rise in consumerism (patients actually want to know what is going on with their treatment and be involved in decisions about their oral care) and the restrictions in funding of healthcare.

Thus an understanding of finance for the dentist and the whole dental practice is becoming a necessity rather than a luxury. Many dentists find finance an irritation in their lives, something they are happy to delegate to the accountant or financial adviser. As a consequence they may hand over the control of their business to someone who understands finance but who probably lacks an understanding of dentistry, and sometimes things go horribly wrong. Remember, the only person responsible when things do go wrong is the dentist, and it can be very expensive.

Basic principles

There are a number of basic financial principles that are so simple they can sometimes be ignored (but ignored at your peril). The first (and most basic) is the financial flowchart (Figure 1.1). Money basically comes to you (in the form of income, gifts, investments, etc) and you spend it (to eat, live and enjoy yourself). As long as this equation balances (or even better more is coming in than going out) then you have some degree of control over money. Once the equation topples into the right hand side (more is being spent than is coming in) then you have real problems.

Fig. 1.1 The financial flowchart

I have collected the factors that effect your financial health in Figure 1.2. They apply equally to you as an individual or to your business.

- Attitude towards money
- Time to think about finances
- An understanding of accounts
- A plan for collecting knowledge
- A willingness to work on yourself

Fig. 1.2 Factors that affect your financial health

Attitude towards money

The first principle is your attitude towards money. If you feel money is impossible to control or that things will 'turn out all right in the end' then you may be heading for trouble. Your attitude towards finance will affect everything you do, which in turn will affect what happens to you. I cannot stress too highly this vital fact.

For example, if you feel that money is a 'dirty word' and you should not have to deal with it then you will ignore possible opportunities to improve the financial health of both you and your staff. If you feel that you should not earn above a certain limit (you put a mental ceiling on your personal income level) then you will ignore opportunities for expansion of your business (unless you are really enlightened and insist on drawing a modest salary and putting all additional profit back into the business). If you feel that people will not value your services (or worse you do not value them yourself) you will seriously limit your earning potential. Figure 1.3 gives a fictional example of this.

Case history

Jane Jones is a dentist working in her own practice in a rural village. She enjoys her work, but has always hated the business aspects of dentistry and would much rather work in a salaried position (if she could find someone prepared to pay her the level of salary she wants). As she could not find a salaried job she purchased her own practice three years ago. She wants to develop her practice into a more specialist practice providing quality (and expensive) dental care.

She has a fairly low self image of herself as a dentist and as a consequence finds it difficult to believe patients in the village will value her dentistry. She suspects most people expect dentistry for free from the State, and even those that are prepared to pay do so reluctantly. She also suspects they only come to see her for convenience and would rather visit a private (and expensive) dentist in the town when they want to pay privately for dental care.

Consequently, she often does not bother to explain to patients some of the expensive private options available to them—because she 'knows' they could not afford it, and even if they could they would probably not want her to provide the treatment herself but refer them to the specialist in the town.

In effect, she is creating the very situation she is afraid of. This becomes a self-fulfilling prophecy, reinforcing her belief.

Her attitude to both herself and money are creating a situation that is definitely to her disadvantage, but naturally she does not appreciate it. So deep is this belief system that it is unlikely she would believe it if someone explained it to her. Her only chance to break the cycle is to trust that she may be wrong in her beliefs and test it—which requires great courage as it goes against her basic feelings. However, if she can overcome her own fears and simply offer these expensive treatment choices to patients (when indicated) she may find she is wrong in her assumptions.

Fig. 1.3 An example of a scenario in practice demonstrating how attitudes towards finance can influence the growth of a dental practice

Time to think about finances

One reason why money controls people so often is because they do not bother to set aside time to think about it. People fail to plan, and as a consequence find themselves going in directions they would prefer not to.

Financial planning is essential. You need to have a financial strategy. This means working out the broad direction of your practice and the broad objectives you wish to achieve. You should be answering questions like:

- What level of financial return do I expect from my practice?
- How much do I want to earn for myself?
- What type of remuneration systems do I want to choose?
- What will be my gross turnover and gross profit margin?
- What percentage of my profit will I invest in my business?

To achieve these objectives you will need a strategy and specific targets as well as a plan for monitoring your progress and achieving your targets. All of this takes both time and thought. You can involve your financial advisers, but remember that it is *your* practice and you should be the one making the basic decisions. You cannot expect an accountant to make the strategic decisions for your business, but you can expect him to advise you on how to achieve them.

An understanding of accounts

Imagine trying to drive to a distant location with no idea of how to read a map, or trying to tune a new television with no instruction book. Although we jokingly say 'When all else fails—read the instructions' we know that many things in life are much easier when you understand how to do them by referring to the instruction book or manual. Now imagine learning to drive or play tennis by yourself with no input from a tutor or coach. You would never know what you were doing right or wrong, or more importantly if you were capable of improvement. You require feedback to enable you to correct your mistakes and improve.

Accounts fulfil both the functions I have described above. They act as an instruction manual telling you what needs to be done (financially) and they monitor your business progress enabling you to correct your mistakes and improve your business. But, unless you can read them, you will not be able to access all this valuable information. Reading *and understanding* financial accounts is not something you can delegate to others, including your accountant. You need a fairly good understanding yourself, not only of how to read accounts but also which items of information are relevant and important.

A plan for collecting knowledge

Knowledge is essential for any business person, but few people actively plan to acquire the right knowledge to equip them for success. Knowledge can only come from one source—other people—but you can develop a plan that will accelerate the process of acquiring it. For example you can attend seminars and training courses, you can read books and journals, you can watch programmes on video and television, and you can just talk to people. The important thing is to have a plan and to put that plan into action.

Willingness to work on yourself

My final factor is probably the hardest of all. Most people look for the easy way, for the quick answer, for the instant solution. Yet acquiring the right knowledge is not easy, nor is the ability to challenge your own beliefs.

Of course this principle does not just apply to finance, but it plays a very large part in your success. If you expect your financial advisers to sort out your finances you may be in for a nasty surprise one day when your business develops real problems. If you think you can leave the book-keeping and accounting of your business to people you pay to do it for you then you will let it run out of control (however adept and supportive they are). If you expect to attend a course on financial planning and come away with all your problems solved you are creating unrealistic expectations. The bottom line is you have to work at developing your financial expertise over a period of time, and you have to keep going.

The myth of working harder

My final principle in this section is the myth that financial difficulties simply mean you need to get your head down and work hard for a few months until you are out of the problem, then revert back to the way things were. This is a stop-gap solution that might work a couple of times, but is it really the best solution? Figure 1.4 illustrates this approach, whereas Figure 1.5 shows the correct way of solving the problem.

You must analyse the situation (using the financial tools you have available and additional help from experts if required) and then take appropriate action. In some cases this may include working harder for a

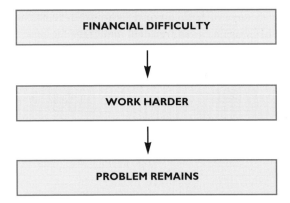

Fig. 1.4 The misconception of how to solve financial difficulties

spell, but this will be part of a proactive approach to solving your problem rather than a reactive measure without any real thought.

Having looked in rather broad terms at a few of the basic principles behind financial planning I would now like to look at a concept I feel underlies much of the financial problems that hinder dental practice and prevent most dentists from reaching their potential.

Dentist as sole trader

In many countries the dentist is a sole trader or partner in a practice, not the managing director of a limited company or a corporation (which in

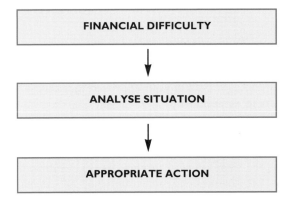

Fig. 1.5 The correct way to solve financial difficulties

law have an identity of their own, separate from their owners). Thus dentists tend to have a 'small business mentality' because they are the owners of small businesses.

There are advantages and disadvantages to this. The main disadvantage is that sole traders tend to think of all the money in the business as being their own personal money (probably because a lot of it is) and this tends to make them more inclined towards cost-cutting than to focus on improving income. Investment in marketing, development of the people in the practice and in themselves is often ignored or downgraded in an attempt to maximise their profits (which they think of as personal income).

In financial terms it would be far better if dentists took out a salary from the practice like the rest of the staff, and considered any excess profits made to belong to the business for further investment and expansion. This would free their minds from the 'it's my money' mentality to 'it's the practice's money' mentality. I am aware that in some countries actually doing this might have tax implications, but I am talking about the concept rather than the reality. You may not actually have to employ yourself but you can always think of your salary in these terms.

Besides this basic approach to finance, sole traders often lack the discipline that owners of limited companies are obliged to use to organise their finances. Regular budget meetings, monthly accounting meetings, planning meetings and auditing of accounts are all part of the corporation or limited company. If dentists could adopt some of these practices (as I explain later in the book) then they would find their control (and ultimately their financial success) would improve.

Finally, I would like to introduce the first financial model in the book—net worth. I am considering it here because (i) it is an easy one to start with, (ii) it combines both personal and business finances, (iii) it forms the basis of where you are now in financial terms, and (iv) because you need occasionally to measure your net worth to check you are following the right path in your approach to business as well as to personal financial management.

Net worth

Net worth is the term for what you are worth if you sold everything you had, paid off all your debts, and counted up how much money was left. It is a fairly simple financial calculation (Figure 1.6) and one worth carrying out at intervals. Net worth can be highly significant if business

	£	£
ASSETS		
Main residence	100,000	
Less mortgage	70,000	30,000
Second residence	30,000	
Less mortgage	15,000	15,000
Contents of both homes		30,000
Car		10,000
Cash:		
Bank		0
Building Society		2,600
Investments		12,000
Life assurance cash values		4,500
Business assets less liabilities		30,000
Other		1,200
TOTAL ASSETS		135,300
LIABILITIES		
Personal loans	7,000	
Bank overdraft	3,000	
Hire purchase agreements	12,000	
Credit cards	3,000	
Tax owing	15,000	
TOTAL LIABILITIES	40,000	
NET WORTH		95,300

Fig. 1.6   Calculation of net worth

is going badly. Negative net worth is the situation where you would be left still owing money if you sold everything you owned to pay off all your debts and then found there was not enough. This is called insolvency and technically means you are personally bankrupt. Few people become personally bankrupt, but many businesses can reach this situation by over-borrowing or over-trading. If this should happen to you then you must take advice fairly swiftly, as you are trading illegally if you continue to carry on your business once you are aware of a negative net worth.

Other things to watch for when calculating net worth are:

- a realistic estimate of goodwill (what would you really get for goodwill if you had to sell your practice now?);
- the true cash-in values of life policies and pension plans (often far less than you fondly imagine);
- the value of property assuming you had to sell in a hurry;
- an accurate estimate of the value of cars, belongings and surgery equipment;
- a realistic view of debts owed to you.

Net worth is also useful if you would have inheritance tax liabilities should you die now, as it can give you an idea of how much the tax would be. Net worth is often used by banks and other financial institutions when they are assessing the risk of lending you money.

Although it is a simple concept, net worth can be very valuable and can warn you of impending problems, or alternatively when things look good, make you feel even better about your situation.

Conclusion

This chapter has introduced some basic financial principles as well as indicating what is to come later in the book. I cannot stress too strongly the importance of your attitude towards money as the key factor in your success at both managing your finances as well as improving your financial health.

2

Profit, loss and balance sheets

An essential part of business finance is about recording and monitoring the various financial transactions, and about knowing the answers to some basic questions that are vital to the health of the business. Ideally you should be fully aware of your financial situation all the time, or at least of the data that will give you quick answers to basic questions.

The basic questions

The most basic questions you need to be able to answer are:

- Where are we now?
- How have we been doing so far?

These can be broken down further into:

- How much money does the business have and where is it?
- Is the money in the business shrinking or growing?

The answers to these basic questions can be found by looking at two familiar documents produced by the accountant—the balance sheet and the profit and loss accounts (P & L) as illustrated in Figure 2.1.

Fig. 2.1 Answering the basic questions using the balance sheet and profit and loss account

The profit and loss account

Most dentists have a better understanding of the profit and loss account than the balance sheet, because it is easier to understand. The P & L shows how much money has come into the practice (income) and how much has been spent (expenditure) in the current period (usually a maximum of a year). The profit is the extra money the business has made (in other words, the excess of money taken in sales over money spent in operating the business).

The P & L only shows money spent on running the business, so it does not show the cost of purchase of any capital expenditure (money spent on buying equipment and other major capital purchases) but will include any interest or fees paid on loan capital and share capital (as these are part of running the business).

Thus the P & L only provides part of the picture of the business, and should not be read in isolation. By just looking at the P & L, you only get an idea of the 'wealth' of the business when it is operating, in other words—is it providing a good profit or not? To get a realistic picture of the financial health of your business you must look at the balance sheet as well.

We will be looking at P & L sheets in more depth in Chapter 3.

The balance sheet

The balance sheet generally provides you with information about how much the business is worth at the time, taking into account all the years it has operated. This includes the amount of cash the business has and where it is in terms of assets purchased, money owed to it and money owed to others. Balance sheets can look quite mystifying until you understand them. The best way of understanding one is to take a simple example of a start-up dental practice and follow its progression through to the end of the first year.

Defining terms

Before starting however, I need to define some financial terms that appear on a balance sheet:

Assets: things that are worth something to the business. These are usually considered as fixed assets (things that are 'fixed' to the business such as equipment, premises, etc) and current assets (things that can easily be removed, such as cash and stock).

Liabilities: things that are claimable against the business and need paying off at some time. These are usually divided into long-term liabilities (such as a mortgage or loan over several years) and current liabilities (things that have to be paid off within a year—such as an overdraft or creditors).

Debtors: people who owe the business money, such as patients, any government or insurance fee system, and money owing from private patient schemes.

Creditors: people who the business owes money to, such as dental laboratories, dental supply houses and the bank.

Working capital: money invested in running the business.

Starting up capital

Most businesses need finance to get started. An analysis of the balance sheet will tell you how much money was required to get the business going, where it came from, and what it has been spent on.

Figure 2.2 shows the basics of money coming into and leaving the business. Most business owners put up some money themselves (share capital) and borrow some money (loan capital). Once a business is up and running it should make enough profit to have some left over, after tax and the owner's income have been paid. This is referred to as reserves. Obviously this money would not appear on the balance sheet of a newly-started company, as it has to wait for some profit to be made. On the other side of the balance sheet, money is spent on buying necessary equipment and premises (assets) and providing working capital to keep the business running (cash and the things purchased with it). Balance sheets can often look different because of the way that

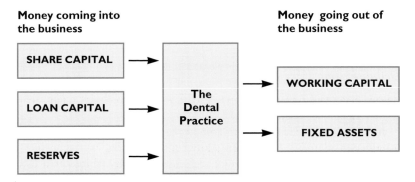

Fig. 2.2   Money going into and leaving the business

accountants choose to draw them up. The simplest structure is like the one illustrated in Figure 2.3(a)—showing a balance between the capital, liabilities and profit and the actual assets of the business. This type of balance sheet balances where the money is now (the assets) with where it came from (capital plus liabilities) plus what you have earned (profit).

However, most accountants prefer the format shown in Figure 2.3(b), which balances what money you have (assets) less the money you owe (liabilities) with what you put into the business (capital), plus what you have earned (profit). The term capital account is often used to describe the capital and profit, and represents what would be left if the owners sold all their assets and paid off their liabilities. In other words, it represents what the owners have got in the business in financial terms.

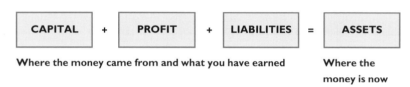

Where the money came from and what you have earned   Where the money is now

Fig. 2.3(a) Balance sheet balancing assets with capital plus liabilities plus profit

What you have less what you owe   What you earn plus what you put in

Fig. 2.3(b) Traditional balance sheet balancing assets less liabilities with capital plus profit

The following imaginary scenario describes the development of a new practice through the balance sheet and profit and loss account. It is simplified to keep the principles clear.

Miss Smith and Mr Jones decide to set up their own dental practice. They each put £2,500 from their own savings into the practice bank account (see Figure 2.4).

Most balance sheets are written as a single column so the accountant would represent this transaction as in Figure 2.5. The capital account, representing the owners' money, is a liability to the business (the practice owes Smith and Jones £2,500 each).

Having placed their money in the bank, Smith and Jones borrow a

Where the money came from	£	Where the money is now	£
SHARE CAPITAL		CURRENT ASSETS	
Savings	5,000	Cash	5,000
Total	5,000	Total	5,000

Fig. 2.4 Smith and Jones: injection of savings

	£
ASSETS	
Bank account	5,000
Total net assets	5,000
Financed by:	
Capital accounts	
Smith	2,500
Jones	2,500
	5,000

Fig. 2.5 Smith and Jones: balance sheet after injection of savings

mortgage of £50,000 to purchase some premises, and purchase some equipment using hire purchase (HP) for £10,000 to put second-hand equipment into the surgeries (for the sake of simplicity, I am ignoring the costs of plumbing in the equipment etc). The simple financial balance now looks like that in Figure 2.6 and the accounts balance sheet is shown in Figure 2.7. Note that the capital account is not affected by the purchase of premises and equipment. Note also that total net assets balances with the capital accounts.

Smith and Jones now draw £2,000 out of the practice bank account to buy stock and £2,000 to improve the fixtures and fittings. This movement of money changes the balance sheet (see Figure 2.8) although the balance remains the same. This is because no new money has been introduced into the business. The right hand side shows the increase in fixed assets and the new split of current assets into cash and

Where the money came from	£	Where the money is now	£
SHARE CAPITAL		FIXED ASSETS	
Savings	5,000	Premises	50,000
		Equipment	10,000
LOAN CAPITAL			
Mortgage	50,000	CURRENT ASSETS	
HP on equipment	10,000	Cash	5,000
Total	65,000	Total	65,000

Fig. 2.6 Smith and Jones: borrowing on mortgage and purchase of premises and equipment

	£
ASSETS	
Bank account	5,000
Premises	50,000
Equipment	10,000
	65,000
LIABILITIES	
Mortgage	(50,000)
HP	(10,000)
	(60,000)
Total net assets	5,000
Financed by:	
Capital accounts	
Smith	2,500
Jones	2,500
	5,000

Fig. 2.7 Smith and Jones: balance sheet after borrowing and purchases

stock. The balance sheet in the accounts (the version the accountant provides) now looks like that in Figure 2.9. Note that the capital account is still not affected by the movement of money between the bank and purchase of assets and things required by working capital.

Where the money came from	£	Where the money is now	£
SHARE CAPITAL		FIXED ASSETS	
Savings	5,000	Premises	50,000
		Equipment	10,000
LOAN CAPITAL		Fixtures/fittings	2,000
Mortgage	50,000		
HP on equipment	10,000	CURRENT ASSETS	
		Stock	2,000
		Cash	1,000
Total	65,000	Total	65,000

Fig. 2.8 Smith and Jones: drawings to buy stock and improve fixtures and fittings

	£
ASSETS	
Bank account	1,000
Premises	50,000
Equipment	10,000
Fixtures/fittings	2,000
Stock	2,000
	65,000
LIABILITIES	
Mortgage	(50,000)
HP	(10,000)
	(60,000)
Total net assets	5,000
Financed by:	
Capital accounts	
Smith	2,500
Jones	2,500
	5,000

Fig. 2.9 Smith and Jones: balance sheet after drawings for stock and improvements

A month later

Although businesses would not normally track their finances via a balance sheet more often than once a year, we can follow this particular case further by looking at what happens to the balance sheet once the business starts to operate.

After a month, Smith and Jones have received £2,000 in patients' fees and paid out £1,000 in expenses. This leaves them with £1,000 profit which enters the balance sheet on the left (new money coming into the business). This money has been banked, adding to the cash in the current assets side (the right side) of the sheet. Now the simple format of our balance sheet looks like that in Figure 2.10.

Where the money came from	£	Where the money is now	£
SHARE CAPITAL		FIXED ASSETS	
Savings	5,000	Premises	50,000
		Equipment	10,000
LOAN CAPITAL		Fixtures/fittings	2,000
Mortgage	50,000		
HP on equipment	10,000	CURRENT ASSETS	
		Stock	2,000
Profit	1,000	Cash	2,000
Total	66,000	Total	66,000

Fig. 2.10 Smith and Jones: first month position with receipt of fees and payment of expenses

On the usual format of a single column (Figure 2.11), the profit has been placed into the capital account (as £500 for each partner) and is balanced by an increase in the bank account in the assets section.

The final transaction in our story is the removal of some of their money by both Smith and Jones, who need it for their own living costs. If we assume each withdraws £1,500 to live on and £500 for tax, then each will remove £2,000 which will reduce the capital account by £4,000 to £2,000 in total (it had increased to £6,000 following the addition of the profit). Normally the balance sheet would not record the withdrawal of money for tax, but simply record total withdrawals.

	£
ASSETS	
Bank account	2,000
Premises	50,000
Equipment	10,000
Fixtures/fittings	2,000
Stock	2,000
	66,000
LIABILITIES	
Mortgage	(50,000)
HP	(10,000)
	(60,000)
Total net assets	6,000
Financed by:	
Capital accounts	
Smith	3,000
Jones	3,000
	6,000

Fig. 2.11 Smith and Jones: balance sheet showing first month position

Figure 2.12 shows the capital account for either Smith or Jones. The total accounts would obviously show both, but most dental practices show accounts for each dentist separately.

	£
CAPITAL ACCOUNT	
Opening balance	2,500
Share of profit	500
	3,000
Cash drawings	(1,500)
Income tax	(500)
	(2,000)
Closing balance	1,000

Fig. 2.12 Smith and Jones: capital account after personal drawings

At the end of the year

We can now look at both the profit and loss account and the balance sheet for Smith and Jones at the end of their first trading year.

The P & L (see Figure 2.13) could refer to the whole practice, but is more likely to refer to the individual dentist. In this case, Smith has earned £70,000 in fees, and her expenses have produced a profit of £26,000 in her first year. Note that the loan interest and bank charges are recorded as these are operating costs, but the P & L does not include capital expenditure (purchase of equipment, car, etc) or loan and share capital.

Note also the figure for depreciation. This is an allowance in the expenditure for money to be set aside to purchase new equipment when the old equipment needs replacing. I will cover the mysteries of depreciation in Chapter 4.

The balance sheet for the whole practice is now shown in Figure 2.14 and has a slightly new format as the totals for each column have been moved one column to the right (simply to make reading it easier). For

	£
INCOME	70,000
EXPENSES	
Materials	10,000
Laboratory fees	7,000
Wages	12,500
Services	3,000
Rates	2,000
Other	3,000
Loan interest	2,000
Bank charges	1,000
Accountant	2,000
Depreciation	1,000
Insurance	500
Total	44,000
PROFIT	26,000

Fig. 2.13 Smith and Jones: profit and loss account at the end of the first trading year

	£	£
ASSETS		
Premises	50,000	
Equipment	10,000	
Fixtures/stock	5,000	
Debtors	1,000	
Goodwill	6,000	72,000
LIABILITIES		
Mortgage	50,000	
HP	10,000	
Creditors	2,000	
Overdraft	2,000	(64,000)
		8,000
CAPITAL ACCOUNT		
Balance at start	5,000	
Profit for year	52,000	
Total	57,000	
Less drawings	49,000	
		8,000

Fig. 2.14 Smith and Jones: balance sheet at the end of the first trading year

simplicity's sake the accounts assume that the value of the premises has not increased and the equipment could be sold off at the same price as it was purchased for. Note that the stock has been included with fixtures, a figure for goodwill has been added, and £1,000 is owed to the practice (debtors) from work carried out but not yet paid for. In contrast the practice now has an overdraft, and owes £2,000 to creditors (probably a combination of dental supplies and laboratory items received but not yet paid for).

The capital account assumes each dentist has made a profit of £26,000 and the total drawings is £49,000. Thus, if everything is kept equal, each will have withdrawn £24,500 to live on (including tax) leaving £8,000 in the total capital account as reserves.

As already mentioned, each dentist would probably have a separate balance sheet and P & L as each would have different circumstances.

Conclusion

This chapter has explained the broad principles of the two main account documents for any business, the balance sheet and profit and loss account. An understanding of both will tell you how your business is doing (is it making money or losing money?) and how the money invested in the business, by both you and those who have lent the business money, has been spent.

3

Using the profit and loss account

In Chapter 2 I looked at two of the basic financial tools that every business owner has, the profit and loss account (P & L) and the balance sheet. In this chapter I will explain how to use these two tools to gather more information—for example, information that can help you to decide whether to purchase a new practice or buy into one, or to analyse your current financial situation when making future strategic choices.

To retrace what was said in Chapter 2, both the P & L and the balance sheet give you information about the financial situation of your practice now. The P & L examines the last 12 months and the balance sheet provides a view of the current 'wealth' of the business on the day it was drawn up. The balance sheet provides information on where the money to set up and run the business came from, how much money will be required to pay off external creditors, and how much would be left for the owners of the business.

Basic analysis

However, we can obtain far more information from these financial tools if we know how to read them. This means we understand what we need to look at, what calculations we may need to do, and what that actually means. This can be expressed as:

- choosing the figures that interest you;
- making any calculations required;
- interpreting the findings.

Figure 3.1 illustrates a simple example of this process. You can use a spreadsheet to perform quite sophisticated analyses if you want, expressing the findings as graphs or pie charts. The principle is the same.

There are two basic ways of looking at this kind of information:

- examining the trend;
- benchmarking.

Case history

Harry Allnet owns a single-handed dental practice. He wants to gain some information from his profit and loss accounts. He follows the three steps of analysis by:

1. deciding he wants to examine the profit of the practice (he could have chosen the gross income or the total expenditure, or just one item of expenditure);

2. looking at this profit over the last three years and comparing the figures with each other—they show a slight decrease in his profit in actual terms compared with inflation;

3. deciding that the figures show a declining trend in profit, which requires some management decisions.

Fig. 3.1 The process of analysing financial information

Examining the trend simply means comparing figures over a period of time, and will be covered more extensively later in this chapter. Benchmarking compares something (such as the profit, or the bad debt figure, or the daily earning) with the same figure at a different moment in time, or with the same figure for a different business or individual. Thus you could compare the daily gross income for a hygienist today with the figure she grossed yesterday, or the same day last week or last month. You could also compare this figure with the daily gross of another hygienist (whether in your own practice or elsewhere). Once you begin analysing accounts you begin to see their real value, as I will demonstrate in this chapter.

P & L percentages

One of the simplest ways of getting more information from the figures on the P & L is to compare the percentages of the items of income and expenditure, either with national averages or over a period of time. Figure 3.2 shows a typical P & L for a mythical practice which is making a profit of £33,084 (all figures represent English pounds but are for illustration only and are applicable for any currency).

Obviously this information is valuable, but if the current year's figures are compared with the previous year's (see Figure 3.3) then a great deal more information can be gained.

For example, net fees (income) have reduced slightly but direct

	1998/99	
GROSS FEES	173,474	
Less associates' remuneration	57,191	
NET FEES	116,283	
Less expenses		
DIRECT EXPENSES		
Materials and drugs	13,478	
Wages and salaries	27,348	
Laboratory expenses	18,854	
Course fees	540	
	60,220	60,220
ESTABLISHMENT EXPENSES		
Rent	8,302	
Rates	700	
Light and heat	1,032	
Repairs and maintenance	146	
Insurance	733	
	10,913	10,913
GENERAL EXPENSES		
Motor and travelling	2,503	
Telephone	1,080	
Printing, postage	932	
Stationery	642	
Accountancy fees	1,450	
Sundry expenses	1,143	
	7,750	7,750
FINANCIAL EXPENSES		
Bank charges & interest	2,503	
Loan interest (equipment)	890	
Hire purchase (car)	1,662	
Bad debts	1,342	
	6,397	6,397
DEPRECIATION		
Fixtures and equipment	2,560	
Motor vehicle	3,109	
	5,669	5,669
TOTAL OVERHEADS		83,199
NET PROFIT FOR YEAR		33,084

Fig. 3.2   Profit and loss account for year ended December 1999

	1998/99		1997/98	
GROSS FEES	173,474		172,271	
Less associates' remuneration	57,191		54,577	
NET FEES	116,283		117,694	
Less expenses				
DIRECT EXPENSES				
Materials and drugs	13,478		11,004	
Wages and salaries	27,348		25,507	
Laboratory expenses	18,854		16,692	
Course fees	540		200	
	60,220	60,220	53,403	53,403
ESTABLISHMENT EXPENSES				
Rent	8,302		8,302	
Rates	700		650	
Light and heat	1,032		984	
Repairs and maintenance	146		102	
Insurance	733		620	
	10,913	10,913	10,658	10,658
GENERAL EXPENSES				
Motor and travelling	2,503		2,850	
Telephone	1,080		926	
Printing, postage	932		703	
Stationery	642		496	
Accountancy fees	1,450		1,380	
Sundry expenses	1,143		742	
	7,750	7,750	7,097	7,097
FINANCIAL EXPENSES				
Bank charges & interest	2,503		2,846	
Loan interest (equipment)	890		1,040	
Hire purchase (car)	1,662		1,662	
Bad debts	1,342		1,586	
	6,397	6,397	7,134	7,134
DEPRECIATION				
Fixtures and equipment	2,560		2,560	
Motor vehicle	3,109		3,582	
	5,669	5,669	6,142	6,142
TOTAL OVERHEADS		83,199		77,337
NET PROFIT FOR YEAR		33,084		40,357

Fig. 3.3 Profit and loss account for year ended December 1999 (with 1998 figures included)

expenses have increased. This may be linked to a change in associate, a different treatment philosophy, a change in staff, or an external change (for example a worsening economic climate or a large company moving away from the area and depressing employment). Most of the other figures have increased in line with expectations, and it is good to see the bad debt figure reducing. There are other inferences to be drawn from the figures, but the main point I want to make here is that a comparison between the most recent year and the year before is far more valuable than simply considering the most recent figures alone.

Figure 3.4 introduces more information for us to consider. It shows the percentage figure for each item when compared with the total overheads for the year. Showing the figures this way makes it much easier to see which outgoings have increased and which have decreased. You can now see from the P & L that wages and salaries have not increased as a ratio, but that materials and laboratory fees have. There are no great surprises in these figures, but those in Figure 3.5 show something very interesting.

Figure 3.5 compares the actual percentages of our example practice with the average national practice figures produced by the Inland Revenue (for the United Kingdom). Our practice is in line with most of the average figures, except for laboratory expenses. The practice might have a good reason for the high laboratory percentage (a specialist crown and bridge practice for example). The point here is not to suggest the Inland Revenue figures are 'right' but to make the practice owner aware of any differences. He can then take the appropriate action if there is no obvious reason for the difference. Thus we can see that refining the P & L provides us with a lot more information than it would if we were simply to look at each year as a list of figures.

What the P & L will not tell you

The P & L will tell you:

- how much money was spent;
- what the money was spent on;
- how the business is doing.

What the P & L will not tell you is:

- how the costs relate to fees (you do not know which items of treatment are more profitable than others);
- how your investment compares with investing elsewhere (if you

	1998/99	%	1997/98	%
GROSS FEES	173,474		172,271	
Less associates' remuneration	57,191		54,577	
NET FEES	116,283		117,694	
Less expenses				
DIRECT EXPENSES				
Materials and drugs	13,478	16.2%	11,004	14.2%
Wages and salaries	27,348	32.9%	25,507	33.0%
Laboratory expenses	18,854	22.7%	16,692	21.6%
Course fees	540	0.6%	200	0.3%
	60,220		53,403	
ESTABLISHMENT EXPENSES				
Rent	8,302	10.0%	8,302	10.7%
Rates	700	0.8%	650	0.8%
Light and heat	1,032	1.2%	984	1.3%
Repairs and maintenance	146	0.2%	102	0.1%
Insurance	733	0.9%	620	0.8%
	10,913		10,658	
GENERAL EXPENSES				
Motor and travelling	2,503	3.0%	2,850	3.7%
Telephone	1,080	1.3%	926	1.2%
Printing, postage	932	1.1%	703	0.9%
Stationery	642	0.8%	496	0.6%
Accountancy fees	1,450	1.7%	1,380	1.8%
Sundry expenses	1,143	1.4%	742	1.0%
	7,750		7,097	
FINANCIAL EXPENSES				
Bank charges & interest	2,503	3.0%	2,846	3.7%
Loan interest (equipment)	890	1.1%	1,040	1.3%
Hire purchase (car)	1,662	2.0%	1,662	2.1%
Bad debts	1,342	1.6%	1,586	2.1%
	6,397		7,134	
DEPRECIATION				
Fixtures and equipment	2,560		2,560	
Motor vehicle	3,109		3,582	
	5,669		6,142	
TOTAL OVERHEADS	83,199		77,337	
NET PROFIT FOR YEAR	33,084		40,357	

Fig. 3.4 Profit and loss account for year ended December 1999 (with 1998 figures included) showing percentage differences between 1998 and 1999

	1999/98		%	Average %
GROSS FEES	173,474			
Less associates' remuneration	57,191			
NET FEES	116,283			
Less expenses				
DIRECT EXPENSES				
Materials and drugs	13,478		16.2%	18.0%
Wages and salaries	27,348		32.9%	34.0%
Laboratory expenses	18,854		22.7%	15.0%
Course fees	540		0.6%	
	60,220	60,220		
ESTABLISHMENT EXPENSES				
Rent	8,302		10.0%	11.0%
Rates	700		0.8%	
Light and heat	1,032		1.2%	
Repairs and maintenance	146		0.2%	
Insurance	733		0.9%	
	10,913	10,913		
GENERAL EXPENSES				
Motor and travelling	2,503		3.0%	
Telephone	1,080		1.3%	
Printing, postage	932		1.1%	
Stationery	642		0.8%	
Accountancy fees	1,450		1.7%	
Sundry expenses	1,143		1.4%	
	7,750	7,750		
FINANCIAL EXPENSES				
Bank charges & interest	2,503		3.0%	
Loan interest (equipment)	890		1.1%	
Hire purchase (car)	1,662		2.0%	
Bad debts	1,342		1.6%	
	6,397	6,397		
DEPRECIATION				
Fixtures and equipment	2,560			
Motor vehicle	3,109			
	5,669	5,669		
TOTAL OVERHEADS		83,199		
NET PROFIT FOR YEAR		33,084		

Fig. 3.5 Profit and loss account for year ended December 1999, comparing percentages with national average

have invested heavily in a superbly equipped surgery, is this bringing in a suitable financial return?);

- where your profit is (is the money available as cash for you to spend or is it committed to repaying loans?);
- what commitments you have in the future (will you need to re-equip soon because your equipment is now worth virtually nothing and is out of date?);
- what the long-term trends are (you may know the difference between this year and last year, but what has been happening over the long term?).

Some of this information is available from the balance sheet, as I described in the last chapter.

The balance sheet

The balance sheet gives you a basic understanding of where the money to finance the practice has come from (the owner's investment, loans from banks and leasing companies, mortgages, etc) and where the money is now (in assets such as premises and equipment, in the bank or as liabilities such as various loans owed to creditors).

However, you need to interpret balance sheets with a degree of caution and understand the way that the numbers can be analysed to produce ratios. These ratios are useful because you can gain more value from them than from the figures alone.

One way to illustrate this is to consider three practices (A, B and C) and their accounts. Figure 3.6 gives a thumbnail sketch of each practice, and as you can see the three are very different.

If you compare the P & L figures and the balance sheets for the three practices, several points are fairly obvious (summarised below).

Practice A represents an average practice, with moderately high borrowing commitments and a slightly low profit compared with average. Despite this, Dentist A is drawing out more than the practice strictly allows to maintain her standard of living.

Practice B appears to be a successful practice on first looking at the figures, as the profits are higher than average, the gross is high and the practice pays a very high wages bill. Dentist B is not taking out too much money for his private drawings (it would seem).

Practice C is earning the least, producing the least profit and also living beyond his means (for this year at least). However the practice owes very little as the loans are now paid off.

Practice A

Dentist A works with a part-time associate in a country practice. Both are average earners, with an average amount of conservation. There is a £40,000 mortgage on the building, well-equipped surgeries and the property is worth £51,000.

A has fairly high loans for the equipment and for redecoration of the house to attract more patients. The practice overdraft is currently running at £2,000.

A has a reasonable profit, but is currently living beyond her means (profit £26,900 – drawings £29,500).

Balance Sheet				**Profit & Loss Account**		
	£	£			£	£
FIXED ASSETS	FEES			FEES		73,800
Buildings	51,000			DIRECT EXPENSES		
Equipment	5,000			Materials	4,600	
Instruments	2,000			Wages	21,400	
Goodwill	5,000			Lab fees	5,300	
		63,000		Course fees	400	
Less mortgage		40,000			31,700	
		23,000				
CURRENT ASSETS				OTHER EXPENSES		
Stock	1,900			Rates	5,300	
Debtors	2,000			Car	2,000	
		3,900		Sundry other	2,300	
				Repairs	600	
CURRENT LIABILITIES					10,200	
Bank loan	(6,000)					
HP loan	(15,000)			FINANCIAL EXPENSES		
Creditors	(1,500)			Bank charges	600	
Bank overdraft	(2,000)			Interest	1,400	
		(24,500)			2,000	
		2,400		DEPRECIATION		
CAPITAL ACCOUNT				Fixtures	2,000	
Balance at start	5,000			Car	1,000	
Profit for year	26,900				3,000	
	31,900					
Less drawings	29,500			TOTAL OVERHEADS		46,900
		2,400		NET PROFIT		26,900

Fig. 3.6A Practices A, B, and C: in financial terms, which practice is best?

Fig. 3.6B and C continued overleaf

Practice B

Dentist B rents rooms in the city and has a plush, well-equipped practice with three associates. He has high expenses (wages of £65,000 and a lab bill of £18,000) but a corresponding high gross (£176,000).

He has borrowed heavily with a £10,800 overdraft and a bank loan to help re-equip, and the high depreciation figure reflects the expensive equipment and fast car. Despite all this, he is living well within his means.

Balance Sheet

	£	£
FIXED ASSETS		
Buildings	0	
Equipment	23,800	
Instruments	6,110	
Goodwill	55,000	
		84,910
Less mortgage		0
		84,910
CURRENT ASSETS		
Stock	3,500	
Debtors	4,000	
		7,500
CURRENT LIABILITIES		
Bank loan	(30,000)	
HP loan	0	
Creditors	(4,500)	
Bank overdraft	(10,800)	
	(45,300)	
		47,110
CAPITAL ACCOUNT		
Balance at start	40,000	
Profit for year	55,110	
	95,110	
Less drawings	48,000	
		47,110

Profit & Loss Account

	£	£
FEES		176,000
DIRECT EXPENSES		
Materials	8,400	
Wages	65,000	
Lab fees	18,000	
Course fees	90	
	91,490	
OTHER EXPENSES		
Rates	7,800	
Car	6,200	
Sundry other	3,700	
Repairs	600	
	18,300	
FINANCIAL EXPENSES		
Bank charges	1,600	
Interest	2,100	
	3,700	
DEPRECIATION		
Fixtures	4,600	
Car	2,800	
	7,400	
TOTAL OVERHEADS		120,890
NET PROFIT		55,110

In financial terms, which is best? Which would be the one to buy from the viewpoint of investing your money?

Anyone purchasing a practice would obviously consider many other aspects besides the finances, such as the patient potential, marketing opportunities in the area, personal requirements (schools for children, etc). Despite this, the following analysis of these examples may provide some interesting and unexpected results that illustrate the added value that can be obtained by looking deeper into the financial accounts.

Practice C

Dentist C is heading towards retirement. He works single-handed with a nurse and part-time receptionist and has paid off all his loans. His equipment and car need replacing, but he feels no necessity to replace either.

He has a profit of £21,000 and has drawn out £24,000 to allow him to take his wife on the holiday they always promised each other while the children were growing up.

Balance Sheet

	£	£
FIXED ASSETS		
Buildings	50,000	
Equipment	1,000	
Instruments	200	
Goodwill	0	
		51,200
Less mortgage		30,000
		21,200
CURRENT ASSETS		
Stock	300	
Debtors	1,000	
		1,300
CURRENT LIABILITIES		
Bank loan	0	
HP loan	0	
Creditors	(1,000)	
Bank overdraft	(700)	
		(1,700)
		20,800
CAPITAL ACCOUNT		
Balance at start	24,000	
Profit for year	21,000	
	45,000	
Less drawings	24,200	
		20,800

Profit & Loss Account

	£	£
FEES		48,400
DIRECT EXPENSES		
Materials	2,400	
Wages	14,700	
Lab fees	4,800	
Course fees	200	
	22,100	
OTHER EXPENSES		
Rates	700	
Car	1,400	
Sundry other	1,500	
Repairs	700	
	4,300	
FINANCIAL EXPENSES		
Bank charges	0	
Interest	0	
	0	
DEPRECIATION		
Fixtures	400	
Car	600	
	1,000	
TOTAL OVERHEADS		27,400
NET PROFIT		21,000

Financial ratios

Financial ratios are simply ratios of various figures to provide information that may not be immediately apparent. Before looking at some ratios I would like to rearrange the balance sheets for Practices A, B and C to make things easier for us to understand. There is no difficulty with writing balance sheets in different ways as long as you understand that you are simply writing the same information in a different format.

For our purposes (rather than for the convenience of the accountant or by tradition) I would like to look at the way the money in the business is being used (or the operating assets) balanced against the sources of the money. Figure 3.7a illustrates this. On the left side of the figure you can see the original balance sheet for Practice A. On the right side the figures have been rearranged. All I have done is move the liabilities (except for the creditors) into the lower part of the balance

Use of the money

	£	£		£	£
FIXED ASSETS			FIXED ASSETS		
Buildings	51,000		Buildings	51,000	
Equipment	5,000		Equipment	5,000	
Instruments	2,000		Instruments	2,000	
Goodwill	5,000		Goodwill	5,000	
		63,000			63,000
Less mortgage		(40,000)			
		23,000	WORKING CAPITAL		
			Stock	1,900	
CURRENT ASSETS			Debtors	2,000	
Stock	1,900		Creditors	(1,500)	
Debtors	2,000				2,400
		3,900			
			Net Operating Assets		65,400
CURRENT LIABILITIES					
Bank loan	(6,000)				
HP loan	(15,000)		**Funding Structure**		
Creditors	(1,500)				
Bank overdraft	(2,000)		Debt		
		(24,500)	Bank loan	6,000	
		2,400	HP loan	15,000	
			Bank overdraft	2,000	
			Mortgage	40,000	
CAPITAL ACCOUNT					63,000
Balance at start	5,000				
Profit for year	26,900				
	31,900		Capital Account	31,900	
less drawings	(29,500)		less drawings	(29,500)	
		2,400			2,400
			Total		65,400

Fig. 3.7(a)   Practice A: traditional balance sheet compared with balance sheet showing use of money and funding structure

sheet. The amount the practice owes to the creditors has been retained in a section referred to as **working capital**, which you will remember from the previous chapter is the money required to keep the business operating.

Figures 3.7b and 3.7c show how the same operation has been performed on Practices B and C. We are now ready to look at how we can use these figures to analyse the ratios.

There are a considerable number of different ratios that you can use to determine how well your business is doing, but for our purpose I

Use of the money					
	£	£		£	£
FIXED ASSETS			FIXED ASSETS		
Buildings	0		Buildings	0	
Equipment	23,800		Equipment	23,800	
Instruments	6,110		Instruments	6,110	
Goodwill	55,000		Goodwill	55,000	
		84,910			84,910
Less mortgage		0			
		84,910	WORKING CAPITAL		
			Stock	3,500	
CURRENT ASSETS			Debtors	4,000	
Stock	3,500		Creditors	(4,500)	
Debtors	4,000				3,000
		7,500			
			Net Operating Assets		87,910
CURRENT LIABILITIES					
Bank loan	(30,000)				
HP loan	0		**Funding Structure**		
Creditors	(4,500)				
Bank overdraft	(10,800)		Debt		
		(45,300)	Bank loan	30,000	
		47,110	HP loan	0	
			Bank overdraft	10,800	
CAPITAL ACCOUNT			Mortgage	0	
Balance at start	40,000				40,800
Profit for year	55,110				
	95,110		Capital Account	95,110	
less drawings	(48,000)		less drawings	(48,000)	
		47,110			47,110
			Total		87,910

Fig. 3.7(b)   Practice B: traditional balance sheet compared with balance sheet showing use of money and funding structure

Use of the money					
	£	£		£	£
FIXED ASSETS			FIXED ASSETS		
Buildings	50,000		Buildings	50,000	
Equipment	1,000		Equipment	1,000	
Instruments	200		Instruments	200	
Goodwill	0		Goodwill	0	
		51,200			51,200
Less mortgage		(30,000)			
		21,200	WORKING CAPITAL		
			Stock	300	
CURRENT ASSETS			Debtors	1,000	
Stock	300		Creditors	(1,000)	
Debtors	1,000				300
		1,300			
			Net Operating Assets		51,500
CURRENT LIABILITIES					
Bank loan	0				
HP loan	0		**Funding Structure**		
Creditors	(1,000)				
Bank overdraft	(700)		Debt		
		(1,700)	Bank loan	0	
		20,800	HP loan	0	
			Bank overdraft	700	
CAPITAL ACCOUNT			Mortgage	30,000	
Balance at start	24,000				30,700
Profit for year	21,000				
	45,000		Capital Account	45,000	
less drawings	(24,200)		less drawings	(24,200)	
		20,800			20,800
			Total		51,500

Fig. 3.7(c)   Practice C: traditional balance sheet compared with balance sheet showing use of money and funding structure

will look at five. Finally I will look at one very important scenario—what would happen if the bank called the overdraft in?

The five ratios are:

- return on capital employed (ROCE);
- return on income;
- return on expenditure;
- overheads costs compared with fees;
- debt to total funding.

Every business would like to feel it is both profitable and successful. Simply looking at profits compared with expenses or income is dangerous, because it can produce a misleading picture. For example, in our three practices A, B, and C, it might be tempting to believe that Practice B is the most profitable—after all, the owner is definitely taking home the most profit and the practice has the highest turnover. Let us see what the ratios show.

Return on capital employed

Figure 3.8a looks at one of the most important ratios, the return on capital employed (ROCE). This figure shows how well the capital invested in the business is doing, and can be compared with putting the money into a building society or investing on the stock market. The reason for the rearrangement of the balance sheet becomes apparent, as the capital employed is easily identified as the net operating assets. As we suspected, Practice B has the best return (63%) which compares very favourably with investing in a building society. If a business's return on investment ratio was low, the owner would need a good reason for investing in a business which is providing a poor return, when financially it would have been better to invest elsewhere.

Return on income ratio

This ratio shows what the return is in financial terms compared with income (in other words how much profit is being made from sales of dental treatment). Figure 3.8b shows us that, despite appearances, Practice C is the most profitable here. However, all three have fairly good ratios.

Return on expenditure ratio

Figure 3.8c now looks at return on expenditure—how profits compare with the costs of producing those profits. Again, all three are reasonable, but the ratio for Practice C is way ahead of the other two. The implication here is that the smaller practice is producing more profit per £1 spent, which is hardly surprising as this practice has low overheads.

Overheads compared with income

This ratio is also an interesting one, as it looks at how much of every £1 earned is being spent on overheads. For the purpose of this ratio we need to remove the depreciation figure (I will explain more about

(a) Return on capital employed

	Practice A	Practice B	Practice C
	£	£	£
Profit	26,900	55,110	21,000
Net operating assets	65,400	87,910	51,500
Return on capital employed	41%	63%	41%

(b) Return on income

	Practice A	Practice B	Practice C
Profit	26,900	55,110	21,000
Income	73,800	176,000	48,400
Return on income	36%	31%	43%

(c) Return on expenditure

	Practice A	Practice B	Practice C
Profit	26,900	55,110	21,000
Expenditure	46,900	120,890	27,400
Return on expenditure	57%	46%	77%

Fig. 3.8 Ratios of Practices A, B and C for return on capital employed, return on income and return on expenditure

depreciation in Chapter 4) to give us a more accurate assessment of what is really happening.

Figure 3.9a shows that C is spending 55p in every £1 on expenses, A is spending 59p and B is spending the most at 64p per £1. This information is perhaps to be expected but can still be valuable as it focuses the mind on the need to ensure that expenses are controlled and monitored, especially over time.

Debt to total funding

This ratio is again fairly obvious when investigated, as it shows how much of the total funding of the practice is made up of debt. Most dental practices do have a high debt ratio, and Figure 3.9b illustrates this. Perhaps the surprising information is that Practice A is the worst and Practice B the best—but this is because Practice B is renting the surgery.

The overdraft

Finally, consider how the three practices would fare if the bank decided to call the overdraft in. Without wishing to be alarmist, this is an action

(a) Spent on overheads

	Practice A	Practice B	Practice C
	£	£	£
Expenditure	43,900	113,490	26,400
Fees	73,800	176,000	48,400
Expenses per £1	59p	64p	55p

(b) Debt to total funding ratio

	Practice A	Practice B	Practice C
Debt	63,000	40,800	30,700
Total funding	65,400	87,910	51,500
Debt to total funding ratio	96%	46%	60%

(c) What would happen if the bank called the overdraft in?

	Practice A	Practice B	Practice C
Overdraft	2,000	10,800	700
Current assets	3,900	7,500	1,300
Overdraft called in	51%	144%	54%

Fig. 3.9   Ratios of practices A, B and C for overheads, debt to total funding and position if overdraft called in

that any bank is totally within its rights to do, and occasionally banks can and do take this action with very little warning. A new manager, a change in banking policy, a lack of communication from the practice or a change in external circumstances (such as a change in government funding or the economic climate) could all result in this action, and it is important for the practice to know how it would manage.

Figure 3.9c shows us what would happen. Practice A would only have to clear 51% of its current assets to find the money, Practice C would have to find 54% (although the overdraft is so small it is hardly worth worrying about) but Practice B has a larger overdraft than its assets cover. Even if B sold all the current assets there would still be money owing, requiring B to sell some fixed assets (such as the car) if the practice could not find a further loan elsewhere. Even if B were to take out another loan, the terms of that loan could be unfavourable because B is not in a good position to negotiate.

Trends

The final part of this analysis is to consider any of the above ratios looked at as trends. Suppose Practice B analyses the debt to total funding ratio over the last five years and noticed a trend for this to be increasing (due to continuing equipment purchases) then he might decide to watch his purchasing more closely for a while to ensure it did not get out of hand. As I stated earlier trends are often more valuable than anything else, and these ratios can all provide you with invaluable information when recorded over a period of time.

Conclusion

The balance sheet and P & L can be extremely useful and valuable sources of information for the owner of a dental practice, and a good understanding of how they work and what they mean is essential for even the most financially terrified.

4

Depreciation

Although many financial concepts are difficult to grasp at first, perhaps the one that seems to confuse people the most is depreciation. This chapter explains what it is and why it is important.

Depreciation can often appear to be a somewhat arcane and mysterious concept that accountants introduce into the accounts to help 'make the books balance' and reduce your tax liability. Very few dentists seem to understand how to use depreciation to help their businesses, or how to make sure the figure your accountant is using is an appropriate, realistic and useful one. First, let us look at the facts, then I will consider the value of including depreciation in your accounts.

What is depreciation?

Depreciation is an allowance for the loss in value of certain items of capital expenditure. Depreciation can often be linked to inflation, because the two work together against you if you need to replace an item of equipment (or other capital expenditure).

In other words, the value of items is reduced because of two factors:

- inflation, which makes it more expensive to purchase the item should it require replacing;
- depreciation, which means an object usually loses value immediately after purchase (if you buy a new car and drive it out of the garage it will have lost a substantial amount of value if you needed to sell it again a few hours later).

The value of depreciation

The value of allowing for depreciation is that it enables you to put aside some money to replace the equipment at an appropriate time. In other words, in an ideal world the amount of money allowed for depreciation in the accounts should be placed into an investment account (or similar

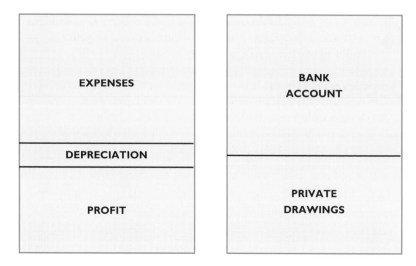

Fig. 4.1 a and b A graphical representation of the significance of putting money aside for depreciation instead of spending it

place) so that when the equipment or car needs replacing the money is there, waiting to be used.

In reality very few people do this. Instead, they take advantage of the depreciation figure to either reduce the overdraft (which is reasonably prudent in times of high interest rates) or, worse, support their lifestyle by spending the money as private drawings. Figure 4.1 illustrates this.

Figure 4.1a represents the profit and loss account, showing the proportion of money required for expenses, the profit and the depreciation. Figure 4.1b contains the same amount of money in the bank, but illustrates that the owner has used part of the amount allowed for depreciation for personal use. You can do this without noticing an increase in the overdraft (or a drain on the amount in the bank) because the depreciation amount allows you to misuse this money without noticing it. This demonstrates quite graphically how it is possible to live on a higher amount of money than the actual profit made in the business without appearing to suffer too much, because the owner is spending money that should be kept in a separate account to replace the equipment at a later date.

While it may be appropriate to do this occasionally (when personal circumstances require it, for example) the danger comes when the individual does not realise what is happening and continues to draw out more money than profits allow. Eventually the need for replacement equipment will require a substantial loan which leads the business into further (and avoidable) debt. Had the owner been more prudent the money would have been available, at least in part.

The real problem is that most dentists are totally unaware of this situation, and are often inadequately advised by their financial adviser who may assume the dentist understands the implications of spending the depreciation allowance and has decided to do it anyway.

Methods of calculating depreciation

The other aspect of depreciation that you should be aware of is the method your accountant uses to calculate the figure. This is more important in times of higher inflation, and an inappropriate method of costing could still lead to problems because the figure is too low and will be inadequate when the new equipment needs purchasing. There are two basic methods of costing for inflation that we need to consider:

- historic costing;
- current costing.

Historic costing

Before the inflationary problems of the 1970s, depreciation was often assessed using the historic cost of the item (Figure 4.2).

To illustrate historic cost, imagine you have just purchased an item of equipment for £10,000 and the life of the equipment is five years.

Original cost of item	£10,000
Year 1: 1/5 of £10,000= £2,000	Depreciation= £2,000
Year 2: 2/5 of £10,000= £4,000	Depreciation= £4,000−£2,000=£2,000
Year 3: 3/5 of £10,000= £6,000	Depreciation= £6,000−£4,000=£2,000
Year 4: 4/5 of £10,000= £8,000	Depreciation= £8,000−£6,000=£2,000
Year 5: 5/5 of £10,000=£10,000	Depreciation=£10,000−£8,000=£2,000
Total	£10,000
Cost of a new item	£15,000
Shortfall	£5,000

Fig. 4.2   Depreciation: historic costing

Using historic costing we simply assume the item is worth nothing five years later, and divide the difference equally by the number of years. Thus in this example each year the item 'loses' the value of £2,000. Figure 4.2 shows us that each year the equipment is worth a proportion of its original (historic) value. The depreciation is the proportion lost less the amount already allowed for.

If you were placing the depreciation amount aside each year in a bank or investment account (in this case £2,000 each year) then in five years time you would have £10,000 ready to purchase a new item of equipment, and as long as inflation was low this figure would be adequate (although almost certainly deficient by a certain amount due to the increase in the price of the equipment). Suppose the equipment actually cost £15,000 five years later then you would have a shortfall of £5,000 even if you had been placing the money aside. Thus the disadvantage of historic costing is that it does not allow for inflation and, were you actually to put the money aside, you would still need to borrow some when purchasing the new item.

Current costing

Current costing avoids the trap of inadequate provision by basing the figure set aside each year on the actual cost of replacing the equipment for that year rather than the historic cost. The calculations are a little more complex, as illustrated in Figure 4.3.

Original cost of item	£10,000	
Year 1: 1/5 of £10,000= £2,000	Depreciation= £2,000	
Year 2: 2/5 of £11,250= £4,500	Depreciation= £4,500−£2,000=£2,500	
Year 3: 3/5 of £12,500= £7,500	Depreciation= £7,500−£4,500=£3,000	
Year 4: 4/5 of £13,750=£11,000	Depreciation=£11,000−£7,500=£3,500	
Year 5: 5/5 of £15,000=£15,000	Depreciation=£15,000−£11,000=£4,000	
Total	£15,000	
Cost of a new item	£15,000	
Shortfall	£0	

Fig. 4.3 Depreciation: current costing

If we assume the item of equipment cost £10,000 on purchase and that it has an expected life of five years, then in Year 1 the depreciation will still be £2,000. However, in Year 2 the price of the equipment has risen to £11,250 and thus the total reduction in value will be two-fifths of £11,250 (£4,500). As we have already allowed for £2,000 in Year 1, the depreciation allowance in Year 2 will be £4,500 less £2,000 which is £2,500. In Year 3 the replacement value of the item of equipment has risen to £12,500. Three-fifths of this is £7,500, so the depreciation figure will be £3,000 (£7,500 less the total amount allowed so far, £4,500).

Following the process through you can see that by the end of the fifth year you will have placed £15,000 into the investment account, and should be able to replace the old equipment with new without borrowing further money. This particular model is quite difficult to understand at first, and needs careful analysis. It is worth making the effort for more expensive items however, as the following example shows.

Figure 4.4 uses the simpler depreciation calculation of allowing for only one-fifth of the current costing each year (instead of the cumulative one-fifth, two-fifths, three-fifths, etc). Although I have used the same finance figures that I used in Figure 4.3, you can see that by using the simpler approach, there is a shortfall of £2,500 at the end of the five years. While Figure 4.4 is a much simpler (and more understandable) calculation it has the disadvantage that the allowance for depreciation falls short of the amount required. This is because the

Original cost of item	£10,000
Year 1: 1/5 of £10,000=£2,000	Depreciation=£2,000
Year 2: 1/5 of £11,250=£2,250	Depreciation=£2,250 (should be £2,500)
Year 3: 1/5 of £12,500=£2,500	Depreciation=£2,500 (should be £3,000)
Year 4: 1/5 of £13,750=£2,750	Depreciation=£2,750 (should be £3,500)
Year 5: 1/5 of £15,000=£3,000	Depreciation=£3,000 (should be £4,000)
Total	£12,500
Cost of a new item	£15,000
Shortfall	£2,500

Fig. 4.4 Depreciation: current costing, alternative version

calculations allow for the increasing replacement value of the item due to inflation, but not for the increasing proportion of that value. In other words, the calculation simply divides the depreciation into fifths and takes one-fifth of the increasing value each year.

Conclusion

In this chapter I have looked at depreciation. Although the basic concept is simple (setting aside money to enable you to replace capital items such as a car or item of dental equipment) the calculations can be complex. The most important point about depreciation is not an understanding of how it is calculated, but the discipline of setting the money aside rather than spending it on other things.

5

Budgets and cash flow forecasts

So far we have tended to look at financial tools that are retrospective because they tell you about your business *after* the event. In this chapter I will look at budgeting, which is the way you plan your finances in advance. One of the most useful forms of budget for the dental practice is the cash flow forecast, so we will look at this in some depth.

Budgeting

Some people find that budgeting is one of those words that produces antagonistic feelings and they try to avoid carrying out any form of budget as long as possible. I suspect that some of the reasons for this are:

- budgets carry a feeling of constriction and control;
- they are believed to be time-consuming and difficult to do;
- life is never the way you think it will be, so why bother?
- budgets just aren't much fun.

Yet budgets are essential in any well-managed business. Not only that, but a managed budget (a budget you use regularly and compare with the actual things that happen) can be very motivational and will help you feel in control.

Budgets and budget forecasts

Before we look at budgeting in the dental practice, I need to clarify terms. A budget forecast is the process of estimating what you think will happen financially over a certain period (usually 12 months). To carry out a forecast you need to estimate your anticipated earnings and the maximum you will spend over the given period.

A budget is the actual financial statement that is drawn up and used as a control over your activities, and is produced from the forecast. It is there to be followed as much as possible, and should be used in the business planning process. For example the budget could assume an

49

Income	£10,000
Expenditure	£60,000
Profit	£40,000

Fig. 5.1 Example of the simplest form of budget

income of £100,000 and an expenditure of £60,000 over a period of 12 months, leaving an anticipated profit of £40,000 (see Figure 5.1). At intervals you check reality against the budget, and if the income is below budget levels or expenditure is higher, then you need to do something to try to bring them back on track.

The importance of the budget is that it acts as a guide to help control expenditure and ensure profit. In Figure 5.2a the income is up by £20,000, which means that profit will also be up—providing expenditure remains within budget. Alternatively, you could decide to keep profit the same and increase expenditure (Figure 5.2b) by investing in the business. However, if income is down (Figure 5.2c) then you might have to forego some of your spending or look at ways of increasing income.

Types of budget forecasts

There are several different types of budget forecasts. A commercial company will often produce a sales budget, an expenditure budget, a capital expenditure budget, a marketing budget and so on. In dentistry we really need to look at a cash flow budget (the movement of cash within the practice); a profit and loss budget (which looks at all the items that will be recorded in the profit and loss statement); a capital expenditure budget (replacement of equipment, car, etc); and a marketing budget (promotion, research into patient views, etc). The essentials of working to a budget are:

- setting financial objectives;
- estimating financial forecasts;
- drawing up the main budget;
- making sure everyone involved knows about it;
- monitoring progress.

Preparing the budget forecasts

There are three main stages in preparing a budget forecast:

- collecting appropriate information;

	Budget	Actual
Income	£100,000	£120,000
Expenditure	£60,000	£60,000
Profit	£40,000	£60,000

(a) Actual income is better than budget, increasing income and profit

	Budget	Actual
Income	£100,000	£120,000
Expenditure	£60,000	£80,000
Profit	£40,000	£40,000

(b) Actual income is better than budget, but so is expenditure

	Budget	Actual
Income	£100,000	£90,000
Expenditure	£60,000	£50,000
Profit	£40,000	£40,000

(c) Decreasing income and expenditure to keep 'within budget'

Fig. 5.2 Budgets used as a guide to control expenditure and increase profit

- working out what you think you will earn;
- working out what you think you will spend.

Collecting information

Information that will affect your budget comes from external and internal factors in the practice, and from something called the 'limiting factor'. This applies to anything that limits your potential to earn. In dentistry it includes any government remuneration system (such as the NHS fee scale in the United Kingdom which you do not control on a day-to-day basis), the location you have chosen (some areas have less potential for private income, some are based on a transient population, etc) and your own practice capabilities (how many dentists you have, the population spread, etc). Thus, dentists in cities may expect a certain level of patient numbers and fee potential that practices in rural areas might not. The types of information you might need to collect are summarised in Figure 5.3. Figure 5.4 illustrates a fictitious example of how budgeting would help a dentist in practice as he plans for his future.

Limiting factors
- Lack of finance to invest
- Expectations of patients to fee scales
- NHS fee scales
- Location of practice
- Local competition

External factors
- Types and number of patients
- Community expectations
- Government policy
- The state of the economy
- Legislation (cross infection control, etc)

Internal factors
- Practice objectives
- Current staffing arrangements
- Condition of equipment

Fig. 5.3   Types of information to collect when forecasting

Estimating income and expenditure

The income flow and expenditure in dental practice will probably remain fairly constant (unless the practice employs a hygienist or increases the number of dentists). Thus estimating income is relatively easy and is likely to be reasonably accurate. One area to be aware of in forecasting expenditure is the difference between direct expenditure (laboratory fees, materials, etc) and indirect expenditure (salaries, electricity, etc). Direct costs tend to fluctuate with workload (and hence income), while indirect costs remain roughly the same regardless of income. The key to good forecasting is in the paperwork, and Figure 5.5 shows an example of the type of form which you could use (obviously you can project figures for the whole year). The most usual method of recording these estimations is called a cash flow forecast.

Cash flow forecasts

A cash flow forecast is really a form of sophisticated budgeting for the business (although you can also apply it to home finances). It will provide you with a calculated guess of the income you think the

Case history

Jim Maitland owns a small dental practice. He works with two expense-sharing associates and one full-time hygienist. His practice philosophy is to develop a preventive-orientated practice offering specialist care in restorative and periodontal dentistry to the local area. For this reason one partner specialises in periodontal care, one in endodontics, and Jim himself specialises in crown and bridge work. The main emphasis so far has been on adult care, although the dentists obviously treat children.

A new housing estate is being developed in the town which is likely to attract families with young children, and Jim decides there is an opportunity to develop the practice by adding paedontics and possibly orthodontics as additional services.

He decides to set up an additional surgery to be shared by a part-time dentist seeing children and a local orthodontist who has already asked if she could work in his practice. Obviously this will require some capital expenditure for the surgery itself, plus a marketing campaign to let people know about the new services offered.

He draws up a marketing budget forecast, and a capital expenditure forecast, and with the help of his accountant integrates these into a profit and loss budget for the next financial year. As a result he estimates he can go ahead with his plans.

Fig. 5.4 An example of long-term budgeting

	January	February	March	April	May
NHS income					
Private income					
Hygienist income					
Toothbrushes					
TOTAL INCOME					

Fig. 5.5 A budget forecast form for income

business will earn and the costs you estimate you will have to pay. Thus you can plan for times when you may need extra funds (an increase on the overdraft perhaps) and work out whether you need to consider increasing income (if possible) or reducing expenditure. You can also estimate a realistic salary for yourself, or see what happens if you draw out more than the business can cope with.

How to develop a cash flow forecast

The simplest way of understanding how to develop a cash flow forecast
is explained in Figures 5.6 to 5.12.

First decide the period for the forecast. Traditionally this would be a
12-month period, January to December. The time span runs across the
top of the model, and the income and expenditure down the left side.
The following figures represent January to June.

The next step is to estimate income figures. These can be all the same

Cash Flow Forecast

	Jan	Feb	Mar	Apr	May	Jun
Balance b/f						
INCOME						
Fees	8,000	7,000	7,000	9,000	10,000	11,000
Other	300	300	300	300	300	300
TOTAL INCOME	8,300	7,300	7,300	9,300	10,300	11,300
FIXED EXPENSES						
Rent & business rates						
Heat & light						
Repairs						
Insurance						
TOTAL FIXED						
RUNNING EXPENSES						
Wages						
Laboratory fees						
Materials						
Bank interest						
Postage						
Telephone						
Accountant						
Other						
Loans						
TOTAL RUNNING						
TOTAL EXPENSES						
PROFIT/LOSS						
Drawings						
Income tax						
BALANCE						

Fig. 5.6 Cash flow forecast: period and income

figure, or in some cases a slight variance based on experience of months that tend to produce higher and lower levels of income because of fluctuations in patient attendance or treatment patterns. In Figure 5.6 I have assumed income is down in February and March (due to seasonal variation).

Having dealt with the income, the next step is to add expenditure. Figure 5.7 shows an example. In this example I have adopted the normal practice of excluding the dentist's income from the wages and added it at

Cash Flow Forecast

	Jan	Feb	Mar	Apr	May	Jun
Balance b/f						
INCOME						
Fees	8,000	7,000	7,000	9,000	10,000	11,000
Other	300	300	300	300	300	300
TOTAL INCOME	8,300	7,300	7,300	9,300	10,300	11,300
FIXED EXPENSES						
Rent & business rates	400	400	400	400	400	400
Heat & light	270		300	270		300
Repairs		125			125	
Insurance			380			
TOTAL FIXED	670	525	1,080	670	525	700
RUNNING EXPENSES						
Wages	1,600	1,600	1,600	1,600	1,600	1,600
Laboratory fees	800	800	800	800	800	800
Materials	250	250	250	250	250	250
Bank interest	50	50	50	50	50	50
Postage	40	40	40	40	40	40
Telephone			330			470
Accountant						
Other	100	100	100	100	100	100
Loans	100	100	100	100	100	100
TOTAL RUNNING	2,940	2,940	3,270	2,940	2,940	3,410
TOTAL EXPENSES	3,610	3,465	4,350	3,610	3,465	4,110
PROFIT/LOSS						
Drawings						
Income tax						
BALANCE						

Fig. 5.7 Cash flow forecast: expenditure

Cash Flow Forecast

	Jan	Feb	Mar	Apr	May	Jun
Balance b/f						
INCOME						
Fees	8,000	7,000	7,000	9,000	10,000	11,000
Other	300	300	300	300	300	300
TOTAL INCOME	8,300	7,300	7,300	9,300	10,300	11,300
FIXED EXPENSES						
Rent & business rates	400	400	400	400	400	400
Heat & light	270		300	270		300
Repairs		125			125	
Insurance			380			
TOTAL FIXED	670	525	1,080	670	525	700
RUNNING EXPENSES						
Wages	1,600	1,600	1,600	1,600	1,600	1,600
Laboratory fees	800	800	800	800	800	800
Materials	250	250	250	250	250	250
Bank interest	50	50	50	50	50	50
Postage	40	40	40	40	40	40
Telephone			330			470
Accountant						
Other	100	100	100	100	100	100
Loans	100	100	100	100	100	100
TOTAL RUNNING	2,940	2,940	3,270	2,940	2,940	3,410
TOTAL EXPENSES	3,610	3,465	4,350	3,610	3,465	4,110
PROFIT/LOSS	4,690	3,835	2,950	5,690	6,835	7,190
Drawings						
Income tax						
BALANCE						

Fig. 5.8   Cash flow forecast: profit and loss for each month

the bottom of the forecast. As I mentioned in Chapter 2 this is less business-like, but is still the norm. The more realistic the figures and the times of payment, the more accurate the forecast.

Figure 5.8 looks at profit or loss for each month, revealing a general trend towards profits. So far things look reasonably healthy, although the profits are not exactly substantial. You could stop the cash flow forecast at this stage if you wanted, but if you continue to take it two further stages you will gain more from the exercise.

Cash Flow Forecast

	Jan	Feb	Mar	Apr	May	Jun
Balance b/f						
INCOME						
Fees	8,000	7,000	7,000	9,000	10,000	11,000
Other	300	300	300	300	300	300
TOTAL INCOME	8,300	7,300	7,300	9,300	10,300	11,300
FIXED EXPENSES						
Rent & business rates	400	400	400	400	400	400
Heat & Light	270		300	270		300
Repairs		125			125	
Insurance			380			
TOTAL FIXED	670	525	1,080	670	525	700
RUNNING EXPENSES						
Wages	1,600	1,600	1,600	1,600	1,600	1,600
Laboratory fees	800	800	800	800	800	800
Materials	250	250	250	250	250	250
Bank interest	50	50	50	50	50	50
Postage	40	40	40	40	40	40
Telephone			330			470
Accountant						
Other	100	100	100	100	100	100
Loans	100	100	100	100	100	100
TOTAL RUNNING	2,940	2,940	3,270	2,940	2,940	3,410
TOTAL EXPENSES	3,610	3,465	4,350	3,610	3,465	4,110
PROFIT/LOSS	4,690	3,835	2,950	5,690	6,835	7,190
Drawings	3,000	3,000	3,000	3,000	3,000	3,000
Income tax	1,000	1,000	1,000	1,000	1,000	1,000
BALANCE	690	(165)	(1,050)	1,690	2,835	3,190

Fig. 5.9 Cash flow forecast: private drawings and allowance for income tax

In Figure 5.9 I have included the private drawings and allowance for income tax. The balance at the bottom of each month simply informs us which month is likely to bring in a profit and which month will result in a loss. By itself this information is useful, but is much more useful when you bring the balance forward to the next month, as we do in Figure 5.10. January's balance is moved to the top of February, and so on throughout the forecast. Note that the balance at the bottom is fairly healthy, apart from a dip in March which seems to be due to an

Cash Flow Forecast

	Jan	Feb	Mar	Apr	May	Jun
Balance b/f	0	690	525	(525)	1,165	4,000
INCOME						
Fees	8,000	7,000	7,000	9,000	10,000	11,000
Other	300	300	300	300	300	300
TOTAL INCOME	8,300	7,300	7,300	9,300	10,300	11,300
FIXED EXPENSES						
Rent & business rates	400	400	400	400	400	400
Heat & Light	270		300	270		300
Repairs		125			125	
Insurance			380			
TOTAL FIXED	670	525	1,080	670	525	700
RUNNING EXPENSES						
Wages	1,600	1,600	1,600	1,600	1,600	1,600
Laboratory fees	800	800	800	800	800	800
Materials	250	250	250	250	250	250
Bank interest	50	50	50	50	50	50
Postage	40	40	40	40	40	40
Telephone			330			470
Accountant						
Other	100	100	100	100	100	100
Loans	100	100	100	100	100	100
TOTAL RUNNING	2,940	2940	3,270	2,940	2.940	3.410
TOTAL EXPENSES	3,610	3,465	4,350	3,690	3,465	4,110
PROFIT/LOSS	4,690	3,835	2.950	5,690	6835	7190
Drawings	3,000	3,000	3,000	3,000	3,000	3,000
Income tax	1,000	1,000	1,000	1,000	1,000	1,000
BALANCE	690	525	(525)	1,165	4,000	7,190

Fig. 5.10   Cash flow forecast: balance brought forward to next month

insurance payment, heat and light bills and the telephone bill all being paid at the same time. On discovering something like this on a cash flow forecast you might decide to convert some of those payments to monthly direct debits to reduce the chance of your bank account slipping into overdraft.

Figure 5.11 demonstrates this by converting the heat and light and telephone bills to monthly payments (I have added a little extra for the

Cash Flow Forecast

	Jan	Feb	Mar	Apr	May	Jun
Balance b/f	0	610	95	(675)	935	3,420
INCOME						
Fees	8,000	7,000	7,000	9,000	10,000	11,000
Other	300	300	300	300	300	300
TOTAL INCOME	8,300	7,300	7,300	9,300	10,300	11,300
FIXED EXPENSES						
Rent & business rates	400	400	400	400	400	400
Heat & light	200	200	200	200	200	200
Repairs		125			125	
Insurance			380			
TOTAL FIXED	600	725	980	600	725	600
RUNNING EXPENSES						
Wages	1,600	1,600	1,600	1,600	1,600	1,600
Laboratory fees	800	800	800	800	800	800
Materials	250	250	250	250	250	250
Bank interest	50	50	50	50	50	50
Postage	40	40	40	40	40	40
Telephone	150	150	150	150	150	1500
Accountant						
Other	100	100	100	100	100	100
Loans	100	100	100	100	100	100
TOTAL RUNNING	3,090	3,815	4,070	3,690	3,815	3,690
TOTAL EXPENSES	3,690	3,815	4,070	3,690	3,815	3,690
PROFIT/LOSS	4,610	3,485	3,230	5,610	6,485	7,610
Drawings	3,000	3,000	3,000	3,000	3,000	3,000
Income tax	1,000	1,000	1,000	1,000	1,000	1,000
BALANCE	610	95	(675)	935	3,240	7,030

Fig. 5.11 Cash flow forecast: utilities' bills converted to monthly payments

interest charges). Note that there is still a financial 'dip' in March, and this exercise might convince you that monthly direct debit payments are not always to your own advantage.

Figure 5.12 takes the forecast one stage nearer to reality by assuming that your bank account is not at zero on 1 January but is actually £4,000 overdrawn. The encouraging news is that, despite this, the cash flow forecast predicts you will be in credit by June. You can enter a similar

Cash Flow Forecast

	Jan	Feb	Mar	Apr	May	Jun
Balance b/f	(4,000)	(3,310)	(3,475)	(4,525)	(2,835)	0
INCOME						
Fees	8,000	7,000	7,000	9,000	10,000	11,000
Other	300	300	300	300	300	300
TOTAL INCOME	8,300	7,300	7,300	9,300	10,300	11,300
FIXED EXPENSES						
Rent & business bates	400	400	400	400	400	400
Heat & light	270		300	270		300
Repairs		125			125	
Insurance			380			
TOTAL FIXED	670	572	1,080	670	525	700
RUNNING EXPENSES						
Wages	1,600	1,600	1,600	1,600	1,600	1,600
Laboratory Fees	800	800	800	800	800	800
Materials	250	250	250	250	250	250
Bank Interest	50	50	50	50	50	50
Postage	40	40	40	40	40	40
Telephone			300			470
Accountant						
Other	100	100	100	100	100	100
Loans	100	100	100	100	100	100
TOTAL RUNNING	2,940	2,940	3,270	2,940	2,940	3,410
TOTAL EXPENSES	3,610	3,465	4,350	3,610	3,465	4,110
PROFIT/LOSS	4,690	3,835	2,950	5,610	5,690	6,835
Drawings	3,000	3,000	3,000	3,000	3,000	3,000
Income tax	1,000	1,000	1,000	1,000	1,000	1,000
BALANCE	(3,310)	(3,475)	(4,525)	(2,835)	0	3,190

Fig. 5.12   Cash flow forecast: beginning the year overdrawn

forecast into your own spreadsheet and try playing around with the figures to see the effects on your business.

Drawing up the budget

Often the type of forecasting likely to cause dental practices the most difficulty lies in the areas of marketing and capital expenditure. The only reason for this is that most practices tend to buy equipment or spend on promotion with little (or no) long-term planning. Obviously

Cash Flow Forecast

	Jan	Feb	Mar	Apr	May	Jun
Balance b/f		£1,890	£2,425	£4,775	£7,365	£9,400
INCOME						
Fees	£10,000	£9,000	£12,000	£11,000	£10,000	£11,000
Other	£300	£300	£300	£300	£300	£300
TOTAL INCOME	£10,300	£9,300	£12,300	£11,300	£10,300	£11,300
FIXED EXPENSES						
Rent & Business Rates	£400	£400	£400	£400	£400	£400
Heat & Light	£270		£300	£270		£300
Repairs		£125			£125	
Insurance			£380			
Accountant		£				
Other	£100	£100	£100	£100	£100	£100
Loans	£100	£100	£100	£100	£100	£100
TOTAL FIXED	£870	£725	£1,280	£870	£725	£900
RUNNING EXPENSES						
Wages	1,600	1,600	1,600	1,600	1,600	1,600
Laboratory Fees	800	800	800	800	800	800
Materials	250	250	250	250	250	250
Bank Interest	50	50	50	50	50	50
Postage	40	40	40	40	40	40
Telephone			330			470
TOTAL RUNNING	£2,740	£2,740	£3,070	£2,740	£2,740	£3,210
Marketing		£500	£800	£300		£1,500
TOTAL EXPENSES	£3,610	£3,965	£5,150	£3,910	£3,465	£5,610
PROFIT/LOSS	£6,690	£5,335	£7,150	£7,390	£6,835	£5,690
Drawings	3,600	3,600	3,600	3,600	3,600	3,600
Income tax	1,200	1,200	1,200	1,200	1,200	1,200
BALANCE	£1,900	£2,425	£4,775	£7,365	£9,400	£10,290

Fig. 5.13   Cash flow forecast incorporating marketing and capital expenditure budgets

it is far better to spend some time thinking about the plans for the practice, estimate what needs to be done to achieve those plans, and budget accordingly. While you could draw up a separate marketing budget and capital expenditure budget, you could also incorporate them into your cash flow forecast as in Figure 5.13. In this example I have assumed some marketing activity in February, March, April and June, and included the figures in the expenditure.

Monitoring the budget

The whole purpose of the budget itself (as opposed to the forecasting) is to act as a financial monitor. Consequently we need to introduce a different paper form that compares budget with actual (see Figure 5.14).

	Budget	Actual	Variance
NHS income			
Private income			
Hygienist income			
Toothbrushes			
TOTAL INCOME			

Fig. 5.14 A monthly budget form

	Jan (budget) £	Jan (actual) £	Variance £
INCOME			
Fees	8,000	8,744	744
Other	300	300	0
TOTAL INCOME	8,300	9,044	744
FIXED EXPENSES			
Rent & business rates	400	400	0
Heat & light	270	299	29
Repairs		54	54
Other	100	26	(74)
Loans	100	100	0
TOTAL FIXED	870	879	9
RUNNING EXPENSES			
Wages	1,600	1,600	0
Laboratory fees	800	647	(153)
Materials	250	230	(20)
Bank interest	50	76	26
Postage	40	26	(14)
TOTAL RUNNING	2,740	2,579	(161)
TOTAL EXPENSES	3,610	3,458	(152)
PROFIT/LOSS	4,690	5,586	896

Fig. 5.15 Cash flow budget

In Figure 5.15 you can see this applied to a cash flow budget on a spreadsheet. Note that in this example the actual income is £744 better than budget, and the expenditure is £161 better. The accounting convention of placing brackets around numbers signifies a minus amount, indicating that expenditure is less than expected, which is better for the business. It starts to become unwieldy to produce long sheets of paper with the budget, actual and variance for every month however, so the convention is to produce a document with the latest month and the year to date (see Figure 5.16).

The time spent in planning a budget is well worth the effort, and if you monitor things regularly it will warn you of events earlier than if you wait for the financial results in your bank statement. Using spreadsheets can also make the process less time-consuming than it used to be in the past.

	Current period		
	(budget)	(actual)	Variance
	£	£	£
INCOME			
Fees	8,000	8,744	744
Other	300	300	0
TOTAL INCOME	8,300	9,044	744
FIXED EXPENSES			
Rent & business rates	400	400	0
Heat & light	270	299	29
Repairs		54	54
Other	100	26	(74)
Loans	100	100	0
TOTAL FIXED	870	879	9
RUNNING EXPENSES			
Wages	1,600	1,600	0
Laboratory fees	800	647	(153)
Materials	250	230	(20)
Bank interest	50	76	26
Postage	40	26	(14)
TOTAL RUNNING	2,740	2,579	(161)
TOTAL EXPENSES	3,610	3,458	(152)
PROFIT/LOSS	4,690	5,586	896

Fig. 5.16a Cash flow budget showing current period.

	(budget)	Year to date (actual)	Variance
	£	£	£
INCOME			
Fees	65,000	69,345	4,345
Other	1,200	753	447
TOTAL INCOME	66,200	70,098	3,898
FIXED EXPENSES			
Rent & business rates	2,000	2,377	377
Heat & light	900	860	(40)
Repairs	600	366	(234)
Other	600	844	244
Loans	1,000	1,000	0
TOTAL FIXED	5,100	5,447	347
RUNNING EXPENSES			
Wages	18,000	17,560	(440)
Laboratory fees	12,000	8,930	(3,070)
Materials	2,000	2,680	680
Bank interest	1,000	1,600	600
Postage	300	580	280
TOTAL RUNNING	33,300	31,350	(1,950)
TOTAL EXPENSES	38,400	36,797	(1,603)
PROFIT/LOSS	27,800	33,301	5,501

Fig. 5.16b   Showing year to date.

Conclusion

Once you begin to appreciate their value then budgets are more likely to be the financial documents you use most of all. It is sensible to have monthly meetings (with business partners or the practice manager) to compare budget with actual, as this enables you to make decisions as to whether to change something (in response to a problem emerging in the budget) or whether to continue in the knowledge you are basically on track.

6

Planning for profitability

The ultimate aim for any business is to make a profit. That is the reason the business exists. This truth can be a difficult one for some professionals to grasp, especially healthcare professionals who have been educated in an environment where the provision of a service was believed to be an end in itself, with no thought of profit for the organisation. Thus dentists can qualify with a very limited view of the financial realities of life, and some would like to continue to practise dentistry (run their businesses) as if this 'fairyland existence' is still appropriate. Unfortunately for them, the fact remains that all businesses exist to make a profit by offering products and services that people want to buy. In this chapter I will look at how you can improve profitability ethically and appropriately.

What is profit?

At first glance this might seem like a stupid question. We all know what financial profit is, and Figure 6.1 illustrates this perfectly.

Profit is what you have left after you have collected all the money owed to you (your income) and paid all your bills (your expenditure). We saw this figure calculated in the profit and loss account in Chapters 2 and 3. Accountants often refer to this type of profit as net profit because it is the 'net' result of the calculation 'income–expenditure'.

For the sole trader or business partner in the United Kingdom the net profit is the amount the Inland Revenue will tax, regardless of the actual amount the dentist will spend on personal drawings for that year.

Fig. 6.1 Calculation of profit

Factors affecting profitability

In an ideal world profit really would be as simple as Figure 6.1. You sell enough business (in other words provide enough professional advice and treatment) and pay your bills and take home the profits (after tax). However, profitability is more complicated than income less expenditure, and as profitability is a necessity we need to consider how to ensure your business is as profitable as possible.

Only three things affect profitability:

- volume;
- price;
- cost.

Again, in its simplest form, the more treatment you 'sell', the more you charge for it and the less you pay out in expenses—the more profit you will make. But few dentists are in business simply to make as much profit as possible, and other factors (such as the quality of your dentistry, the ethical considerations, the quality of life at work and at home, etc) mean that we need to take a balanced view on all this. For this reason, I shall explain some of the basic principles of costing and pricing.

Costing

Costing is the process of working out the costs of producing products and services. In dentistry we are concerned more with costing by the hour or by the treatment item itself, and sometimes with both.

Costing by the hour

This is probably the most common method of costing. The equation is a fairly simple one (Figure 6.2). The total expenses (£56,866) as determined in the profit and loss account or by keeping your books up-to-date and estimating current expenses are divided by the number of hours you have worked. Please note that pricing is not determined by cost plus profit alone, as we will see later.

In the example in Figure 6.2 the total hours worked includes an allowance for days off sick and courses attended, plus holidays, bank holidays, etc. In this example, the practice is costing £35 an hour based on the fixed and variable costs.

		£
Total expenses		£56,866
Number of hours worked in a day	7	
Number of days worked in a week	5	
Number of weeks worked in a year	48	
Total hours worked	1,680	
Less days for sickness	5	
Less days for courses	5	
Total hours subtracted	70	
Total hours worked	1,610	
Cost per hour (expenses/hours worked)		£35

Fig. 6.2 Calculation of costs per hour

Costing with associates

Many practices have dental associates or expense-sharing principals. In some cases the accounts for expense-sharing principals will draw up the costings separately, usually dividing shared expenses that tend to occur outside the individual surgeries separately and including the full cost of the surgery costs to each principal. Associate costings can become more complicated.

Figures 6.3 to 6.8 illustrate this by looking at a typical small dental practice with one principal owner dentist and two associate dentists, A

	Principal	**A**	**B**
	£	£	£
Number of hours worked in a day	7	7	7
Number of days worked in a week	5	5	4.5
Number of weeks worked in a year	48	46	48
Total hours worked	1,680	1,610	1,512
Less days for sickness	5	0	1
Less days for courses	5	10	1
Total hours subtracted	70	70	14
Total hours worked	1,610	1,540	1,498

Fig. 6.3 Calculation of hours for all dentists in the practice

	Total £	Principal £	A £	B £
DIRECT EXPENSES				
Materials and drugs	13,809	4,388	5,766	3,655
Laboratory expenses	18,679	3,655	10,637	4,387
Course fees	2,200	200	2,000	0
	34,688	8,243	18,403	8,042
WAGES AND SALARIES	42,645	14,215	14,215	14,215
ESTABLISHMENT EXPENSES	10,914	3,638	3,638	3,638
GENERAL EXPENSES	7,752	2,584	2,584	2,584
FINANCIAL EXPENSES	6,396	2,132	2,132	2,132
DEPRECIATION	2,559	853	853	853
TOTAL OVERHEADS	104,954	31,665	41,825	31,464

Fig. 6.4 The direct expenses for the three dentists have been calculated according to their individual costs, the other costs divided equally

and B. Figure 6.3 shows the hours worked by the principal, Associate A and Associate B. From these figures we can see that the principal works the most number of hours (1,610 per year), Associate A attends a substantial number of courses in a year, and Associate B attends the barest minimum of courses and works the least number of hours in the practice (the half-day might be a hospital appointment or simply a half-day off).

Figure 6.4 shows the expenses, which have been divided into direct expenses (materials, laboratory expenses and course fees) and different groups of fixed expenses. These have been subdivided into salaries; establishment expenses (rent, mortgage, etc); general expenses (electricity and telephone); financial expenses involving interest repayments and depreciation. The direct expenses have been divided according to the real costs to each dentist, whereas the other expenses have been divided equally.

Figure 6.5 shows what happens when we divide the totals calculated in Figure 6.4 (the overheads of the practice) by the number of hours worked by each of the dentists. This reveals that Associate A is costing the most per hour, mainly due to the very high laboratory fees (due in this case to the fact that Associate A specialises in crown and bridge work). Thus we have calculated the costs per hour for each dentist based on the number of hours worked and a proportion of the overheads.

	Total £	Principal £	A £	B £
DIRECT EXPENSES				
Materials and drugs	13,809	4,388	5,766	3,655
Laboratory expenses	18,679	3,655	10,637	4,387
Course fees	2,200	200	2,000	0
	34,688	8,243	18,403	8,042
WAGES AND SALARIES	42,645	14,215	14,215	14,215
ESTABLISHMENT EXPENSES	10,914	3,638	3,638	3,638
GENERAL EXPENSES	7,752	2,584	2,584	2,584
FINANCIAL EXPENSES	6,396	2,132	2,132	2,132
DEPRECIATION	2,559	853	853	853
TOTAL OVERHEADS	104,954	31,665	41,825	31,464
Number of hours worked		1,610	1,540	1,498
Cost per hour		£19.67	£27.16	£21.00

Fig. 6.5   Costing when wages, establishment, general and financial expenses and depreciation are divided equally

Different types of costing

The problem with the above example is that it only tells part of the story. As managers of the business, we might need to use different types of costing to help us make decisions on pricing, improving profitability, reducing expenditure and other day-to-day decisions that business owners make all the time.

The type of costing we have used so far makes the assumption that the fixed overheads can be divided equally between the three dentists to estimate costs. This type of costing may be referred to as direct costing where the costs that can be directly charged to the service (or product) are set against the service (or product). Direct costing is useful in looking at the most likely scenario that happens in practice, and avoids complicating matters. It is relatively simple to calculate, and reasonably accurate.

But what would happen if one of the associates were to leave and could not be replaced. Although the volume of work would probably increase for the remaining two dentists, the individual costs would also increase (and here we are only considering costs). Figure 6.6 illustrates

	Total £	Principal £	A £
DIRECT EXPENSES			
Materials and drugs	13,809	4,388	5,766
Laboratory expenses	18,679	3,655	10,637
Course fees	2,200	200	2,000
	34,688	8,243	18,403
WAGES AND SALARIES	34,575	17,288	17,288
ESTABLISHMENT EXPENSES	10,914	5,457	5,457
GENERAL EXPENSES	6,348	3,174	3,174
FINANCIAL EXPENSES	6,396	3,198	3,198
DEPRECIATION	2,559	1,280	1,280
TOTAL OVERHEADS	95,480	38,639	48,799
Number of hours worked		1,610	1,540
Cost per hour		**£24.00**	**£31.69**

Fig. 6.6 Costing when one of the associates is not replaced

this, still using a form of direct costing (I have assumed some of the overall overheads would reduce—such as salaries and variable expenses). Now the principal's costs have increased from £19.67 an hour to £24.00 an hour and Associate A's costs have increased from £27.16 an hour to £31.69 an hour. These are considerable increases, especially if taken over a 12-month period.

Suppose the remaining two dentists were to increase their hours worked. This would mean the principal would have to work an extra 1.5 hours per day to reduce the costs to £19.76 an hour (as opposed to £19.67 before Associate B left). Associate A would also need to work an additional 1.25 hours a day to reduce his costs to £26.89 an hour (as opposed to £27.16 an hour). Figure 6.7 shows this.

Of course, all of these costings are theoretical, but they are of value as management accounting tools helping you to manage the business.

One way of helping prepare the financial decision-making process in the case of a change in costings (such as Associate B leaving and no replacement being found) is to adopt a more stringent form of costing with regard to fixed overheads. In Figure 6.8 the costings include the whole amount for each person for establishment and financial expenses and depreciation. Note that the new costings (when compared with

	Total £	Principal £	A £
DIRECT EXPENSES			
Materials and drugs	13,809	4,388	5,766
Laboratory expenses	18,679	3,655	10,637
Course fees	2,200	200	2,000
	34,688	8,243	18,403
WAGES AND SALARIES	34,575	17,288	17,288
ESTABLISHMENT EXPENSES	10,914	5,457	5,457
GENERAL EXPENSES	6,348	3,174	3,174
FINANCIAL EXPENSES	6,396	3,198	3,198
DEPRECIATION	2,559	1,280	1,280
TOTAL OVERHEADS	95,480	38,639	48,799
Number of hours worked		1,955	1,815
Cost per hour		**£19.76**	**£26.89**

Fig. 6.7   The dentists would have to increase their hours to reduce the costings to the original amount. The principal would need to work an extra one and a half hours a day, and Associate A would need to work an extra hour and a quarter a day

Figures 6.4 and 6.5) are close to the increased costings calculated if Associate B left and was not replaced. This type of calculation may cover you if an associate dentist were to leave the practice and could not be replaced. It also may mean you have to adopt a pricing policy (see later in the chapter) which is too high because of other factors such as competitive pricing from other dentists in the area or the perception of your patients as to a maximum value for dentistry.

Costing by product

The other way of costing is to cost by product. This might seem more appropriate for dentures, crowns and other items of treatment where there is an identifiable product, but the costing methods employed in a manufacturing company are not really relevant to a service-driven business such as dentistry. Dental products are so individual that this type of costing does not lend itself easily to mass production calculations.

One form of costing that is often adopted is a blend of costing by the hour and costing by product when laboratory work is involved. Thus

	Total £	Principal £	A £	B £
DIRECT EXPENSES				
Materials and drugs	13,809	4,388	5,766	3,655
Laboratory expenses	18,679	3,655	10,637	4,387
Course fees	2,200	200	2,000	0
	34,688	8,243	18,403	8,042
WAGES AND SALARIES	27,348	9,116	9,116	9,116
ESTABLISHMENT EXPENSES	10,914	**10,914**	**10,914**	**10,914**
GENERAL EXPENSES	7,752	2,584	2,584	2,584
FINANCIAL EXPENSES	6,396	**6,396**	**6,396**	**6,396**
DEPRECIATION	2,559	**2,559**	**2,559**	**2,559**
TOTAL OVERHEADS	89,657	39,812	49,972	39,611
Number of hours worked		1,610	1,540	1,498
Cost per hour		**£24.73**	**£32.45**	**£26.44**

Fig. 6.8 Costing when the total costs for establishment and financial expenses and depreciation are included

the cost of a crown or denture can be calculated as the time involved plus the laboratory fee. If you are using this type of costing then do remember to subtract the laboratory costs from your calculations for hourly rates.

Pricing

Pricing is a vital part of profitability, and may well become even more important to dental practices as various government policies reduce the amount of money available for dentistry in the future. Pricing is also an important aspect for any form of private dentistry. Yet pricing as a topic is usually misrepresented in dentistry.

The common method given for pricing (and the one I feel is incomplete) is that price is expenditure plus profit (Figure 6.9). There

| PRICE | = | EXPENDITURE | + | PROFIT |

Fig. 6.9 A common (but incomplete) equation for pricing

are a number of other factors involved in pricing, although cost is obviously an important element (Figure 6.10). From the customer's point of view you can also add such matters as urgency (people will pay more to get something in a hurry), availability, convenience,

Cost

Obviously the cost of carrying out treatment needs to be considered when looking at pricing. If the price is too low, the treatment could result in a loss, and if this happens too often then the profitability (and viability) of the business is threatened.

Customer expectation

Price is governed by what people expect to pay, and this is often influenced by the price charged by the competition as well as by general expectations. In the United Kingdom dentistry still retains the expectation that dental treatment was 'free' or heavily subsidised by the NHS, and so people often expect to pay very little for healthcare.

The 'going rate'

This is really the price set by the competition, and in some cases can be kept high by operating a form of 'price-fixing' cartel. Usually this situation does not last for long, either due to an aggressive player entering the market or to intervention from the Prices and Monopolies Commission.

Introductory 'offers'

Some dental practices will offer a 'free' consultation or a low initial price for treatment in order to try and persuade people to attend. This practice is fairly common for companies entering a new market to raise awareness, and is usually successful. Care must be taken not to offer lower prices for too long, as profitability obviously suffers.

Bid pricing

Companies making 'bids' for contracts often have to try and calculate the lowest price possible without sacrificing profitability to try and gain the business. Although other factors are involved, bids pricing is usually affected most by the cheapest price getting the contract. The Personal Dental Service (PDS) has brought this type of pricing into the dental market.

Discounts

Discounts are often offered to try and entice people to buy, sometimes by artificially setting prices high so they can be 'discounted' to the intended price anyway. Genuine discounts should be offered with care, as the effect on profitability can be much greater than expected (as explained in Figure 6.11).

Fig. 6.10 Factors that can affect pricing

affordability and so on. The key to pricing is the word 'value'. People will pay more for value, and the dentist's aim should be to find out what patients value as part of the pricing strategy. These topics are more in the realm of marketing than financial management.

Pricing is making sure you get the right price for you and the right price for your patients (getting the balance right). The rest of this section makes the assumption that the practice has control over pricing.

The effect of a price increase and reduction

One of the factors you should be aware of is how a small change in price has a correspondingly greater effect on your profitability. Figure 6.11 shows the effect of increasing and reducing prices by 1% and 5%, and illustrates how the effect can be quite substantial. A tiny increase in price from the customer's point of view is hardly noticed by the person paying for it, yet the effect on your business can be quite impressive. By the same token, a small discount can have a much greater effect on your profitability (a 5% reduction in price reduces your profitability by 13.5%).

1% rise in prices

	Before	After 1% rise in price without losing any sales	After 1% cut in price without losing any sales
	£	£	£
Total income	70,000	70,700	69,300
Total expenditure	44,000	44,000	44,000
Profit	26,000	26,700	25,300
% change in profit		2.69%	−2.69%

5% rise in prices

	Before	After 5% rise in price without losing any sales	After 5% cut in price without losing any sales
Total income	70,000	73,500	66,500
Total expenditure	44,000	44,000	44,000
Profit	26,000	29,500	22,500
% change in profit		13.46%	−13.46%

Fig. 6.11 How a 1% and 5% change in prices will have much higher effect on profit

Classical price theory

Classical price theory states that if you increase prices then you will sell less, and that as you increase the volume of work you sell so the unit cost of providing that work decreases. This results in a graph that looks like Figure 6.12, which shows that at the cheaper price you make less profit because the product brings in less revenue, and at the more expensive end you make less profit because you sell less. Somewhere in the middle is the ideal price for selling the most and obtaining the most profit.

Figure 6.13 illustrates this. I have made some assumptions here to make the point, rather than to try and create a totally believable situation. I would also like to warn readers that this exercise might upset some people who are not yet completely happy with the concept that running a dental practice is running a business. This example aims to demonstrate the effect that pricing can have on your business. It is not intended to suggest this is how you should run your business.

In Figure 6.13 I have looked at pricing for a crown (I have purposely avoided choosing which type of crown). I have assumed that the crown will cost £40 laboratory fee, and that the clinical time taken is one hour at a cost of £35 an hour (this cost excludes laboratory fees). Thus the unit cost per crown is £75. The table illustrates the pricing exercise. The first column shows the possible prices that could be charged in a range from £100 to £500. The next column shows an estimate of the number of crowns you feel people would buy in a year at the proposed price (obviously we assume the crowns are clinically required). This results in column 3—the revenue if that number of patients actually bought

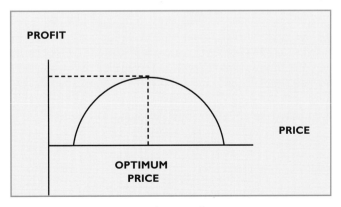

Fig. 6.12 The optimum price for a product

Price of crown	£40			
Hourly cost	£35			
	£75			

Selling price	Probable annual sales	Total revenue	Cost of crown,	Annual profit
£	£	£	£	£
100	300	30,000	22,500	7,500
150	250	37,500	18,750	18,750
200	200	40,000	15,000	25,000
250	150	37,500	11,250	26,250
300	100	30,000	7,500	22,500
350	80	28,000	6,000	22,000
400	50	20,000	3,750	16,250
450	20	9,000	1,500	7,500
500	10	5,000	750	4,250

Fig. 6.13   Calculating the optimum price for a crown

that number of crowns. The next column shows the cost of those crowns at £75 a crown, leaving the final column showing the annual profit. Using this as a guide you can see that the most profitable price to charge is £250, even though you would only provide 150 crowns instead of 300 at the lowest price.

This model is fascinating, but at the same time it obviously does not tell the whole story. Suppose you could not fill the time released by only taking up 150 hours of treatment instead of 300 hours? Would it be more sensible to charge the lower fee to fill the time, or to charge the higher fee and use the time doing something else (like taking time off perhaps)? Suppose you felt it was unethical to make a profit margin of 330%—even though you might make a loss in other areas of treatment? Suppose you got your estimates wrong? Suppose the technician found out what you were charging and felt justified in putting up the prices of crowns?

Pricing, like most things in finance, is more complex than people think.

Volume

The final part of the equation in profitability is volume. I have mentioned it several times already because it is impossible to discuss costs and pricing in isolation. Obviously an increase in the volume of sales will result in increased profits (all other things being equal).

However, volume should be a last resort in improving profitability. Increasing the amount of work you do personally often has repercussions on your performance and your quality of life, for much smaller returns in profitability than you can achieve by taking a careful look at both costing and pricing. I have looked at ways of increasing volume without overdoing personal performance (as well as summarising things you can do in pricing and costs) in Figure 6.14.

Working capital

I have left working capital to the end of the book because it is likely to be the most important factor in improving profitability on a day-to-day basis, and is obviously very important in practices working under a 'fixed prices' system. Thus you can flip open the book at the back whenever you want a reminder of this vital aspect of financial management.

As I discussed in Chapter 2, the balance sheet is a snapshot of the current financial state of your practice. It looks at the money you used to start the business, and at how that money has been spent (or where it is now). Initially, funds for your business can only come from two sources—your own money (share capital) and other people's money (loan capital). You will spend this on assets (such as equipment and stock) and on other items required to get the business going (wages, electricity, insurance, etc). The two aspects combined are known as working capital.

Working capital is the money required to run the business. Put another way—it is the money tied up in your business because you have not yet sold your product or service. Working capital is the money you use (or borrow) to start providing your service, and in theory it will be paid off once you have successfully sold your service to enough people and made enough profit. The problem with working capital is that you cannot stop your business—stop paying the wages, electricity and so on, collect all the money owed to you, pay off the overdraft, and keep the profit. You have to keep going on the working capital cycle so that you can continue to provide your services and keep trading (Figure 6.15).

The cycle works like this:

- On day 1 you use some cash to pay for the services required to provide dental treatment.

Volume
1. Increase work provided for patients
   - Employ more associates/auxiliaries
   - Improve the quality of clinical services
   - Improve the range of clinical services

2. Improve efficiency
   - Open the practice more hours
   - Work shift work
   - Improve layout, or fit more surgeries into the space
   - Reduce non clinical time between patients

Price
1. Increase prices
   - Review prices generally
   - Inflation-proof prices six monthly
   - Surcharge for urgency
   - Surcharge for convenient times
   - Reduce (or eliminate) any form of discounts

2. Increase more profitable treatment
   - Set a direction for your practice
   - Market the practice to the local population
   - Learn how to sell treatment ethically

Cost
1. Reduce direct costs
   - Buy less materials
   - Improve stock control
   - Obtain competitive quotes
   - Negotiate discounts for prompt payment

2. Reduce fixed overheads
   - Sublet space if applicable
   - Spread payments where appropriate
   - Use economic tariffs when possible
   - Negotiate loan interest rates

3. Reduce creditors
   - Ask for payment promptly
   - Spread costs by offering credit
   - Introduce effective bad debt control

4. Improve cash flow
   - Keep treatment courses short
   - Complete paperwork efficiently
   - Pay bills when absolutely necessary

Fig. 6.14 Things you can do to improve profitability

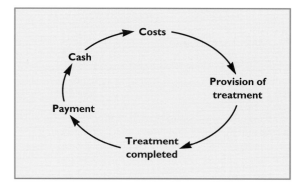

Fig. 6.15 The working capital cycle

- Over the next few days you see some patients and treat them.
- On completion of the treatment you are paid.
- This cash is then used to purchase further services . . . and so on.

This would be fine if everyone paid on time, everything was delivered as expected and the money was banked fast enough to help fund the purchase of new materials and services. However, problems start to occur when the cycle is held up in any way. The longer the delay, the worse the problem, as more and more working capital is required and more of your money is tied up in the system rather than sitting in your bank.

For example, the time between a patient attending for their first visit and completing treatment affects the cycle. In a busy practice this might take two to three months, and if you then have to wait another couple of months before payment in full, then the working capital cycle has lasted between five and six months. For all that time you have been using borrowed money (borrowed from the business if no-one else) rather than the money paid for the service by the patient (or State system). The secret of profitability is in the way you organise and operate your working capital cycle.

The most obvious problem for the small business (in terms of working capital) is the one of demanding suppliers (people who want you to pay them) and tardy customers (people you want to pay you). Fortunately, dental practices are less vulnerable than many other small businesses, as most patients will pay reasonably rapidly and the State payment system is normally guaranteed (albeit sometimes a little slow). Despite this, however, dentists can do several things to reduce their

- Set up forecasting system (cash flow forecast) to anticipate future volumes of work and financial requirements.

- Control purchasing (stock control) to keep costs down. Do not increase stock too much by participating in 'free offer with bulk purchase' promotions.

- Set up an efficient appointment system that reserves treatment times if the period between examination and treatment is getting lengthy.

- Set up efficient clinical systems that enable as much treatment as possible to be done in as few visits as possible.

- Set up a good credit control system, taking payment as early as possible and chasing bad debts as quickly as possible.

Fig. 6.16   Ways to reduce the length of the working capital cycle

working capital, which have encouraging effects on profitability. These are outlined in Figure 6.16.

Conclusion

I have looked at profitability in the dental practice from the aspects of cost, volume and price. Figure 6.14 is a summary of ideas for improving profitability, incorporating some of the ideas throughout the book.

Glossary

Accounting ratios: calculations that allow the figures in accounts to mean something relevant to the running of the business.

Assets: things that are worth something to the business. These are usually considered as fixed assets (things that are 'fixed' to the business such as equipment, premises, etc) and current assets (things that can easily be removed, such as cash and stock).

Balance sheet: statement showing the assets and liabilities at the end of a given period of time, and also how the business has been funded.

Budget: the actual estimate of income earned and expenditure drawn from the budget forecast.

Budget forecast: the expected income and expenditure for the business.

Capital: money to be given to the business by the owners or by banks and other organisations (or individuals) lending the money to the business.

Capital expenditure: money spent on items that have a 'realisable' value (in other words you could sell them).

Cash flow: the movement of money into and out of the business.

Cash flow forecast: the calculation of estimates of income and expenditure over a given time period.

Creditors: people who the business owes money to, such as dental laboratories, dental supply houses and the bank.

Current assets: the name given to items that tend to flow into and out of the business on a daily basis, usually cash and stock.

Current liabilities: short-term debts that need to be settled within a 12-month period.

Debtors: people who owe the business money, such as patients, any government or insurance fee system and money owing from private patient schemes.

Depreciation: the amount of value in financial terms that a fixed asset loses.

Direct cost: any cost directly associated with a service or product.

Direct expenditure: expenditure associated with a service or product, which will vary with the amount of production or activity.

Expenditure: total outgoings.

Fixed assets: the name given to items that the business owns of a more permanent nature, usually equipment and premises.

Fixed costs: the name given to outgoings that occur whether the business is running or not, such as the rent for premises.

Gross profit: profit before tax (in dental terms). (In many businesses this term is reserved for profit after the direct costs have been deducted from the revenue.)

Indirect expenditure: outgoings not linked to the production of products or the activity of the business.

Liabilities: things that are claimable against the business and need paying off at some time.

Limiting factor: an influence on the business's activity that limits trading or pricing, usually used in drawing up a budget.

Loss: a negative value of profit.

Overheads: costs that are not directly associated with the service or product.

Profit and loss account (P & L): statement showing the business income and costs over a period of time, and the resultant profit (money made) or loss (money lost).

Revenue: the value of income earned from all sources (but not necessarily received).

Start-up-expenditure: costs incurred in starting the business for the first time.

Variable costs: costs that occur as a result of sales activity.

Working capital: money invested in running the business.

Index